Data Hiding

This page is intentionally left blank

Data Hiding

Exposing Concealed Data in Multimedia, Operating Systems, Mobile Devices and Network Protocols

Michael Raggo

Chet Hosmer

Wesley McGrew, Technical Editor

AMSTERDAM • BOSTON • HEIDELBERG • LONDON
NEW YORK • OXFORD • PARIS • SAN DIEGO
SAN FRANCISCO • SINGAPORE • SYDNEY • TOKYO

ELSEVIER

Syngress is an Imprint of Elsevier

Acquiring Editor:	Steve Elliot
Development Editor:	Heather Scherer
Project Manager:	Mohanambal Natarajan
Designer:	Joanne Blank

Syngress is an imprint of Elsevier
225 Wyman Street, Waltham, MA 02451, USA

Library of Congress Cataloging-in-Publication Data

Raggo, Michael T.
   Data hiding: exposing concealed data in multimedia, operating systems, mobile devices, and network protocols / Michael T. Raggo and Chet Hosmer. --1st ed.
      p. cm.
   Includes bibliographical references and index.
   ISBN 978-1-59749-743-5 (alk. paper)
1. Computer security. 2. Data protection. I. Hosmer, Chet. II. Title.
QA76.9.A25R3374 2013
005.8--dc23
                                                                                      2012033627

British Library Cataloguing-in-Publication Data
A catalogue record for this book is available from the British Library.

ISBN: 978-1-59749-743-5

Transferred to Digital Printing in 2013

For information on all Syngress publications visit our werbsite at *www.syngress.com*

Dedication

Mike Raggo Dedication

For my Dad (Joe), whose hard work and determination taught me that anything is achievable. Thank you for helping me fulfill my destiny. Also dedicated to the United States Armed Forces and the American Red Cross.

Chet Hosmer Dedication

For my Dad, who shared his stories of using morse code to transfer coded messages onboard the U.S.S. Neosho while serving in the U.S. Navy. After that I was hooked.

```
..-. --- .-.  -- -.--  -.. .- -..  --.-  .-- ..... ---  ... ..... .- .-. . -.. ....
.. ....  ... - --- .-. .. ... ....  --- .-.  .- .... .. -. --.  -- --- .-. ... .  -.-.
--- -.. .  - --  -. .-. .- -. ... .-. .-.  -. .- --- -.. . -..  -- . .... ... .- --.. .
... --- -. .-.. --- .-. -. -..  - ..... .  .- .-. .-.- ... .-.-.- ... .-.-  -. . . ---
.... --- .-- ..... .. .-.  ... . .-. ... .-.- -. --.  .. -.  - ..... .  .- .-. .-.-. ....
.-.-.  -.- .-.- ---.-.- .-.-  .- .-.- - .-. .  - ..... .- -  .. .-- .- ...  ....
--- --- -.- . -.. .-.-.-
```

This page is intentionally left blank

Raggo Acknowledgments

Mike would like to thank the following people and organizations for their inspiration, mentorship, friendship, faith, motivation, and support: Coach Konopka, Warren Bartley, The entire Gibbons Family, Steven Jones, David Thomas, Frank Castaneira, Bill Niester, Taylor Banks and DC404, Michael Hamelin, Gabe Deale, Arnold Harden, BSA, Ronnie James Dio, Renee Beckloff, Jim Christy, Richard Rushing, James Foster, Stratton Sclavos, Michael Schenker, Joel Hart, Todd Nightingale, Amber Schroader, Amit Sinha, Robert Strain, Adam Geller, Fran Rosch, Mark Tognetti, RB Smith, Angelina Ward, Maxx Redwine, Black Hat, DefCon, MISTI, NAISG Atlanta, ISSA, OWASP, PFIC, and The Pentagon.

A big thank you to Robert Wesley McGrew, Heather Scherer, Steve Elliot, and everyone at Syngress.

And Chet Hosmer for his dedication, support, passion, and creativeness in co-authoring the book with me. I couldn't have done it without you, thank you.

And very special thanks to my wife Linda, daughter Sara, and my mom for their unwavering support.

In memory of Joseph Kugler, Maxx Redwine, John Mills, and Chris Blanchard

This page is intentionally left blank

Hosmer Acknowledgments

My sincere thanks go to:

Mike Raggo co-author on this book who brought unique insights along with his organic approach to developing and investigating new data hiding methods.

My whole team at WetStone/Allen who assisted in the validation and experimentation of the latest data hiding threats. Matt Davis, Raghu Menon, Jacob Benjamin, James Bettke, Taylor Hanson, Austin Browder, Bill Fanelli and Carlton Jeffcoat.

A special thanks to the entire team at Syngress especially Steve Elliot and Heather Scherer without their assistance we could have never made this happen.

and, finally to my wife Janet who always provides me daily inspiration no matter how crazy my ideas might be!

This page is intentionally left blank

Contents

About the Authors

MICHAEL T. RAGGO

Michael T. Raggo (CISSP, NSA-IAM, CCSI, SCSA, ACE, CSI) applies over 20 years of security technology experience and evangelism to the technical delivery of Security Solutions. Mr. Raggo's technology experience includes penetration testing, wireless security assessments, compliance assessments, firewall and IDS/IPS deployments, mobile device security, incident response and forensics, and security research, and is a former security trainer. In addition, Mr. Raggo conducts ongoing independent research on various Data Hiding techniques including steganography. Mr. Raggo has presented on various security topics at numerous conferences around the world (Black-Hat, DefCon, SANS, DoD Cyber Crime, OWASP, InfoSec, etc.) and has even briefed the Pentagon on Steganography and Steganalysis techniques.

CHET HOSMER

Chet Hosmer is the Chief Scientist & Sr. Vice President at Allen Corporation and a co-founder of WetStone Technologies, Inc. Chet has been researching and developing technology and training surrounding data hiding, steganography and watermarking for over a decade. He has made numerous appearances to discuss the threat steganography poses including National Public Radio's Kojo Nnamdi show, ABC's Primetime Thursday, NHK Japan, CrimeCrime TechTV and ABC News Australia. He has also been a frequent contributor to technical and news stories relating to steganography and has been interviewed and quoted by IEEE, The New York Times, The Washington Post, Government Computer News, Salon.com and Wired Magazine. Chet also serves as a visiting professor at Utica College where he teaches in the Cybersecurity Graduate program. Chet delivers keynote and plenary talks on various cyber security related topics around the world each year.

This page is intentionally left blank

About the Technical Editor

Wesley McGrew is a research associate at Mississippi State University, where he develops courseware and teaches digital forensics to wounded veterans and members of law enforcement as part of the National Forensics Training Center. He develops new offensive security and digital forensic techniques and tools in both his day job, and in private consultancy as McGrew Security. He has presented at Black Hat USA and Defcon, and has been invited to give talks at many other conferences and events on topics surrounding digital forensics, offensive security, and hacker culture.

This page is intentionally left blank

Preface

It's 4 AM at Spika, a small cramped Internet Café in downtown Prague. A young student is sipping a coffee in the back corner of the café. He enters a blog and posts a photograph with the caption Zhelayu vsego khoroshego or (wishing you the best). At precisely 6 A.M. dozens of Botnet operators visit the same blog page automatically retrieving the photograph posted as instructed. The operators have repeated this operation for months, as done many times before, the bot operators save the image and copy down the caption. They extract the first 8 Fibonacci characters from the caption Zhelayu vsego khoroshego (1,1,2,3,5,8,13,21) that yield "ZZhea oh". Next they load the image into a steganography program named JPHS, and use the Fibonacci extracted pass phrase "ZZhea oh". However, unlike days before, the program asks for the name of a file to store the hidden contents. Normally it rudely reports incorrect pass phrase …. But not today.

As instructed the bot operator's type in "attack.txt" and press Enter. The file "attack.txt" is then created. It contains a simple list of 2,047 IP addresses along with the date of May 9, 2007. The bot operators activate their team of zombies that are spread across the globe dutifully awaiting orders. They provide the attack list and set the attack date to May 9th, 2007. On the morning of May 9th, one of the most wired countries in Europe has instantly become and island, as 100,000+ zombies surgically attack their country's infrastructure with a relentless distributed Denial of Service attack that lasts over a week, thereby isolating this small country 300 miles east of Stockholm. Most of us in the western world have never heard of this country, but it's one we won't soon forget.

The zombies are now asleep, but the bot operators continue to wait for new images with lists of the next victims to attack with their even larger army of zombies.

Obviously, this is a factious and sensationalized rendering of how the cyber attacks on this small but now well-known country of Estonia began. Or is it?

The use of steganography and hidden codes has been part of warfare for over 3,000 years now. The success or failure of missions in many cases depends on the ability to securely and covertly command, control and communicate. When the mission is international espionage, communication with agents abroad, communication within criminal and/or terrorist organizations, or advanced persistent cyber threats, the requirement for this type of communication only increases. The goals of covert communications haven't changed much in the last 3,000 years, however, the methods and techniques continue to evolve as new means of hiding data appear.

Over the past decade data hiding has steadily moved from digital images to multimedia files, then to network protocols, and now Smart mobile devices. As the capabilities of our computing platforms and the bandwidth of our networks increases, and the mobility of our communication device of choice accelerates, so does the means to leak information or covertly communicate anywhere and anytime.

Taking a snap-shot in time, this book examines the trends, latest threats, methods and techniques employed by those hiding data and covertly communicating. The book also examines methods to detect, analyze and uncover such methods, while looking toward the future to extrapolate what might be next.

## CHAPTER 1

History of Secret Writing

INFORMATION IN THIS CHAPTER:

- Introduction
- Cryptology
- Steganography

CONTENTS

INTRODUCTION

Data Hiding transcends nearly every aspect of our daily lives, whether it be for good intent or evil. It stemmed from secret writing thousands of years ago, as cited by David Kahn and many historians. It originated in Egyptian civilization in the form of hieroglyphs, intended as symbolic representations of historical timelines for particular lords. Other cultures of the time, such as the Chinese, took a more physical approach to hiding messages by writing them on silk or paper, rolling it into ball, and covering it with wax to communicate political or military secrets. For added security measures, the ball was even be swallowed during transit. As civilization evolved, forms of covert communications became more sophisticated and cryptograms and anagrams advanced.

David Kahn's The Codebreakers is arguably the most comprehensive historical book about Secret Communications through the ages. Below is a timeline of some of the most notable innovations over the centuries dating back to Egypt and China (see Figure 1.1).

As evident throughout history, secret writing evolved from the need for covert communications. And what is used by our own militaries today to protect us from evil intent, is also used by our enemies to attack our well being. As technology has evolved, so have the ways in which data hiding is used. Today, it is commonly used in corporate espionage, spy communication, malware, child exploitation, and terrorism. Malicious data hiding occurs daily all around us, and many times undetected.

Data Hiding. http://dx.doi.org/10.1016/B978-1-59-749743-5.00001-8

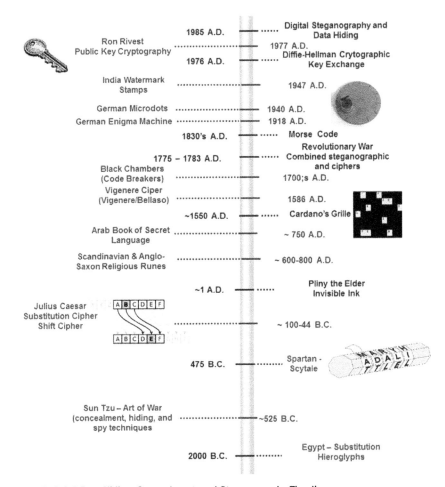

FIGURE 1.1 Data Hiding, Concealment, and Steganography Timeline

In this book we hope to enlighten you, the reader, with information about the many ways in which data hiding is used, from physical mediums to digital mediums. Although there is the ongoing threat of criminal activity, data hiding is actually a very interesting and fun hobby and for some people, a career. Let's begin by reviewing the history behind what brought us to digital data hiding, by reviewing many of the techniques of our ancestors and the basis behind cryptography and steganography.

CRYPTOLOGY

Cryptograms and anagrams are commonly found in newspapers and puzzle books. Cryptograms substitute one character for another. In terms of the alphabet, one letter is substituted for another. The goal of the cryptogram is for the individual to determine what letters are substitutes for others, and use this substitution to reveal the original message. In anagrams, the characters that make-up a message are rearranged rather than substituted.

In either case, the message is made secret by the method or algorithm used to scramble it. There is typically also a key known only to the sender and receiver, such that no one else can read or decipher the message. This secret message is commonly referred to as a cipher text. An eavesdropper cannot read the message unless they determine the algorithm and key. The process of decoding the message is referred to as *cryptanalysis* (see Figure 1.2).

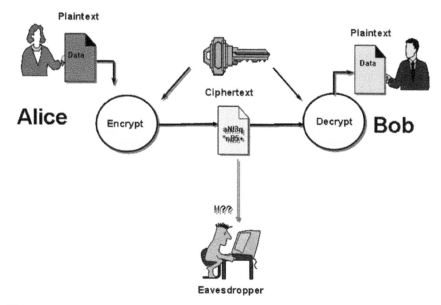

FIGURE 1.2 Cryptography

Substitution Cipher

In cryptography, a substitution cipher is a method of encryption in which plaintext is substituted with cipher text using a particular method or algorithm. The plaintext can be replaced by letters, numbers, symbols, etc. The algorithm defines how the substitution will occur and is based upon a key. Therefore, the recipient of the message must know the algorithm and the key (or keying mechanism) in order to decipher the message. When the recipient receives the encrypted message, he/she will use this known substitution algorithm, to decipher the message to reveal the plaintext message.

Caesar

Julius Caesar (100–44 B.C.) initially created a substitution cipher for military purposes that involved substituting Greek letters for Roman letters, thereby making the message unreadable to the enemy. Caesar later created the more commonly known Shift Cipher. Caesar simply shifted the letters of the alphabet by a specified amount. This shifted alphabet was then used for the substitution cipher. In both cases, the original alphabet was substituted by a different character substitution, also referred to as a cipher alphabet or monoalphabetic cipher. For example:

A B C D E F G H I J K L M N O P Q R S T U V W X Y Z
F G H I J K L M N O P Q R S T U V W X Y Z A B C D E

Using the cipher alphabet we can generate a ciphertext message:

Plaintext Message = STEGANOGRAPHY RULES
Ciphertext Message = XYJLFILWFUMD WZQJX

Although considered a weak cipher by today's standards with the computing power available today, it still exists today primarily in the form of entertainment from everything from newspaper cryptograms to children's secret decoder rings. For example, one of the promotional items from the Johnny Quest cartoon was a secret decoder ring. Children could use the ring to encode secret messages in a substitution cipher format. A little known fact about the decoder ring is that it also included a secret compartment, as well as a sun flasher (see Figure 1.3).

FIGURE 1.3 Johnny Quest Decoder Ring.[1]

Caesar's language substitution cipher approach was also used in WWII by the Navajo code talkers. At the time, the Navajo Indians spoke in a dialect unfamiliar to most other people, including other Indian tribes. As a result, the 29 Navajos were recruited into the Marine Corps to support the war effort. The Marine Corps used the Navajo Code as a secure means of translating English to Navajo for communications while on the battlefield. Since Navajo speak was

---

[1] Johnny quest ring. Stephen A. Kallis, Jr. & Metro Washington Old Time Radio Club.

unknown to anyone except Navajo tribe members and a handful of Americans, it was practically impossible to impersonate.

Coded Radio Messages and Morse Code

In the 1830s, Samuel Morse created a code for sending messages over telegraph. Morse substituted a series of dots and dashes to represent each letter of the alphabet. This code commonly known today as Morse code, was a simple substitution of a character for a letter of the alphabet and punctuation (see Figure 1.4).

An example of the Morse code substitution cipher is used in the Rush song "YYZ." Interestingly enough YYZ is the airport code for Toronto, Canada, Rush's home town. In Morse code, the letter Y is "-. - -" and the letter Z is "- -. ." Coverting YYZ to Morse code you have: YYZ = "-. - - -. - - - -. ." or "dash dot dash dash dash dot dash dash dash dash dot dot." Unbeknownst to most people, this is the basis for the intro to the song.

Some argue that Morse code is not a substitution cipher, because its intentions were not to hide the message, but rather use it as a form of communications at a time when telephone was yet to be invented. Yet it is a form of substitution

A	· —	N	— ·
B	— · · ·	O	— — —
C	— · — ·	P	· — — ·
D	— · ·	Q	— — · —
E	·	R	· — ·
F	· · — ·	S	· · ·
G	— — ·	T	—
H	· · · ·	U	· · —
I	· ·	V	· · · —
J	· — — —	W	· — —
K	— · —	X	— · · —
L	· — · ·	Y	— · — —
M	— —	Z	— — · ·

FIGURE 1.4 Morse Code Table

and represents a form of code substitution. And transposition forms of it were used during the last few wars. In fact, most people listening to the song YYZ have no idea that it even begins with Morse code, thereby making this a form of message hiding (steganography).

Vigenere Cipher

The Vigenere cipher was originally created by a group of intellectuals but was finally organized into a cipher by the fellow whose name it acquired Blaise de Vigenere. Rather than base the substitution on a single alphabet of letters, Vigenere created it based on 26 alphabets (see Figure 1.5).

Using only one column in the Vigenere table would be the equivalent of the Caesar Shift Cipher. Therefore the Vigenere table is designed such that multiple rows

	A	B	C	D	E	F	G	H	I	J	K	L	M	N	O	P	Q	R	S	T	U	V	W	X	Y	Z
A	A	B	C	D	E	F	G	H	I	J	K	L	M	N	O	P	Q	R	S	T	U	V	W	X	Y	Z
B	B	C	D	E	F	G	H	I	J	K	L	M	N	O	P	Q	R	S	T	U	V	W	X	Y	Z	A
C	C	D	E	F	G	H	I	J	K	L	M	N	O	P	Q	R	S	T	U	V	W	X	Y	Z	A	B
D	D	E	F	G	H	I	J	K	L	M	N	O	P	Q	R	S	T	U	V	W	X	Y	Z	A	B	C
E	E	F	G	H	I	J	K	L	M	N	O	P	Q	R	S	T	U	V	W	X	Y	Z	A	B	C	D
F	F	G	H	I	J	K	L	M	N	O	P	Q	R	S	T	U	V	W	X	Y	Z	A	B	C	D	E
G	G	H	I	J	K	L	M	N	O	P	Q	R	S	T	U	V	W	X	Y	Z	A	B	C	D	E	F
H	H	I	J	K	L	M	N	O	P	Q	R	S	T	U	V	W	X	Y	Z	A	B	C	D	E	F	G
I	I	J	K	L	M	N	O	P	Q	R	S	T	U	V	W	X	Y	Z	A	B	C	D	E	F	G	H
J	J	K	L	M	N	O	P	Q	R	S	T	U	V	W	X	Y	Z	A	B	C	D	E	F	G	H	I
K	K	L	M	N	O	P	Q	R	S	T	U	V	W	X	Y	Z	A	B	C	D	E	F	G	H	I	J
L	L	M	N	O	P	Q	R	S	T	U	V	W	X	Y	Z	A	B	C	D	E	F	G	H	I	J	K
M	M	N	O	P	Q	R	S	T	U	V	W	X	Y	Z	A	B	C	D	E	F	G	H	I	J	K	L
N	N	O	P	Q	R	S	T	U	V	W	X	Y	Z	A	B	C	D	E	F	G	H	I	J	K	L	M
O	O	P	Q	R	S	T	U	V	W	X	Y	Z	A	B	C	D	E	F	G	H	I	J	K	L	M	N
P	P	Q	R	S	T	U	V	W	X	Y	Z	A	B	C	D	E	F	G	H	I	J	K	L	M	N	O
Q	Q	R	S	T	U	V	W	X	Y	Z	A	B	C	D	E	F	G	H	I	J	K	L	M	N	O	P
R	R	S	T	U	V	W	X	Y	Z	A	B	C	D	E	F	G	H	I	J	K	L	M	N	O	P	Q
S	S	T	U	V	W	X	Y	Z	A	B	C	D	E	F	G	H	I	J	K	L	M	N	O	P	Q	R
T	T	U	V	W	X	Y	Z	A	B	C	D	E	F	G	H	I	J	K	L	M	N	O	P	Q	R	S
U	U	V	W	X	Y	Z	A	B	C	D	E	F	G	H	I	J	K	L	M	N	O	P	Q	R	S	T
V	V	W	X	Y	Z	A	B	C	D	E	F	G	H	I	J	K	L	M	N	O	P	Q	R	S	T	U
W	W	X	Y	Z	A	B	C	D	E	F	G	H	I	J	K	L	M	N	O	P	Q	R	S	T	U	V
X	X	Y	Z	A	B	C	D	E	F	G	H	I	J	K	L	M	N	O	P	Q	R	S	T	U	V	W
Y	Y	Z	A	B	C	D	E	F	G	H	I	J	K	L	M	N	O	P	Q	R	S	T	U	V	W	X
Z	Z	A	B	C	D	E	F	G	H	I	J	K	L	M	N	O	P	Q	R	S	T	U	V	W	X	Y

FIGURE 1.5 Vigenere Cipher.[2]

---

[2] Fields, B. T. Vigenere cipher photo. Public domain (original author).

are used. A different row is used for each letter to be ciphered. This is performed by assigning a keyword to the ciphering approach. For example, if we chose a keyword of "combo" and use the Vigenere table we could cipher the following message:

Message: thekeyisunderthedoormat
Keyword: combo
Ciphertext: vvqlsawevbfsduvgamu

This form of substitution cipher is known as polyalphabetic, because it uses multiple alphabets to perform the ciphering, as opposed to the monoalphabetic Caesar Shift Cipher. When released, the Vigenere cipher was impenetrable. For example, the Caesar Shift Cipher could be cracked by a cryptanalyst using frequency analysis, whereby certain letters such as e and n are more commonly found in words, whereas x and z not. Understanding this flaw allowed cryptanalysts to decrypt a message. Figure 1.6 outlines English language letter frequency from highest frequency to lowest frequency of occurrence.

High   Medium   Low   Rare
ETAONIRSH DLUCM PFYWGBV JKQXZ
Highest   →   Lowest

FIGURE 1.6 English Language Letter Frequency

In addition to frequency analysis, cryptanalysts also used linguistic characteristics to decipher messages. For example, the combination of "io" appears quite commonly in a word in the English language, whereas the combination of "oi" is rare. Ancient cryptanalysts would actually use lists of letters that are never found together in a word, thus allowing certain combinations to be eliminated immediately. But this assumes that you know the language that the message is written in, which is not always the case. Could it be Spanish, French, or something else? This distinction is critical to the cryptanalyst.

The Vigenere cipher had far more keys in its substitution implementation, making it practically impossible to crack using frequency analysis or linguistic analysis. Vigenere also included the complexity of the vast number of possible keys and key lengths. It is for this reason that the Vigenere cipher endured hundreds of years of secure use until 1854 when Charles Babbage was credited with performing successful cryptanalysis on the Vigenere cipher.[3] Many tools exist today on the web for enciphering messages using the Vigenere cipher. These tools are commonly found on the Internet, thus allowing virtually anyone the ability to encode a message (see Figure 1.7).

---

[3] The Code Book, by Simon Singh, p. 78.

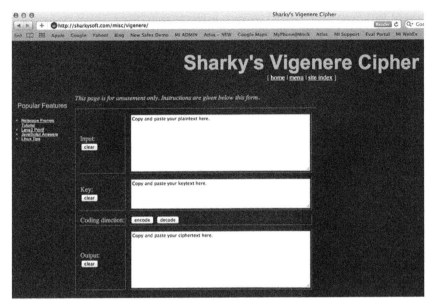

FIGURE 1.7 Internet-based Vigenere Ciphering Tool

Even though the Vigenere cipher is considered inherently weak by today's standards and computing power, it is still found in many ciphering implementations. For example, a hybrid of the Vigenere cipher is used in the Cisco IOS found on routers and other networking devices. Although MD5 (Message Digest Algorithm) hashing is a supported option within the IOS, many Cisco devices still use the Password 7 hashing (a hybrid of the Vigenere cipher). There are a plethora of tools available for decoding the Password 7 hashing for the Cisco IOS. Therefore it is highly recommended that network administrators change the default hashing mechanism from Password 7 to MD5, since the weaknesses in the Vigenere cipher are well known (see Figure 1.8).

Transposition Cipher

Another form of enciphering technique is known as a transposition cipher. This involves rearranging the letters of a plaintext message. The letters themselves remain intact, but are rather simply repositioned. Transposition ciphers are also commonly found in newspapers and puzzle magazines and are commonly referred to as "jumbles" or anagrams. For example,

Hiddenmessage => dihegassemned

These types of transposition ciphers can be relatively easy to crack. So let's take a look at some more complex implementations of transposition ciphers.

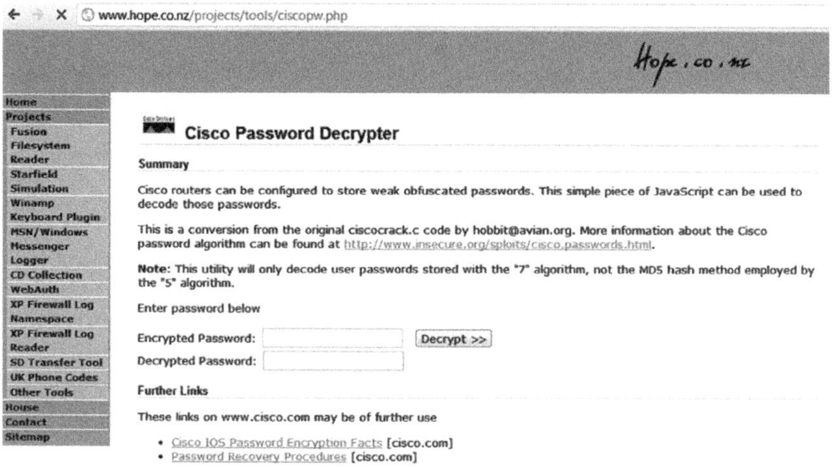

FIGURE 1.8 Online Cisco Password Decrypter.[4]

Spartan Scytale

Probably one of the oldest known implementations of the transposition cipher was the Spartan Scytale (also commonly spelled as Skytale). In ancient Greece (around 475 B.C.), the Spartan army commanders created a Scytale, a device they designed for sending secret messages (Figure 1.9). The army commanders would wrap a strip of parchment or leather around the Scytale wooden staff. They would then write the secret message along the length of the staff. The message would then be unwound from the staff and delivered to another commander. If intercepted by the enemy, the message would be meaningless without the correct size wooden staff, and would appear as a jumble of letters. The receiving commander would then take his identical Scytale and would wrap the message strip around it to reveal the secret message. This repositioning technique is one of the earliest known transposition ciphers.

FIGURE 1.9 Spartan Scytale.[5]

---

[4] Cisco password decrypter—http://www.hope.co.nz/projects/tools/ciscopw.php.
[5] Gualtieri, D. M. Spartan Scytale—http://www.devgualtieri.com.

Repeatedly running a message through a transposition cipher is one way of increasing the complexity of cracking the message, effectively a transposition of a transposition, or as it is commonly known, a *Double Transposition*.

The Difference Between Substitution Ciphers and Transposition Ciphers

Substitution ciphers differ from transposition ciphers. In a transposition cipher, the plaintext is repositioned, but the letters are left unchanged. In contrast, a substitution cipher maintains the same sequence of the plaintext and modifies the letters themselves. As demonstrated earlier, transposition ciphers are limited by their limited principle of repositioning. There's simply only so many ways you can reposition the letters of a message, therefore most of these techniques can be cracked by hand without the necessity for a computer. Substitution ciphers have literally thousands of different implementations, some of which include serious complexity.

Today, the complexity of substitution ciphers has increased tremendously since the creation of the computer. This computing power also allows the ease of combining substitution and transposition into one ciphering technique. For example, Data Encryption Standard (DES) "applies 16 cycles of transposition and substitution to each group of eight letters."[6] Impractical hundreds of years ago, brute-force attacks on keys are also commonplace with today's computing power. Today, the computer is a cryptanalyst's strongest weapon.

STEGANOGRAPHY

Commonly people confuse or overlap the definitions of cryptography and steganography. People commonly refer to steganography as hidden or secret writing, but that's technically incorrect. The difference comes about from the definitions of the Greek word "crypt" versus the greek word "steganos." Or in English terms, the difference between *hidden* writing versus *covered* writing. In cryptography, *hidden* writing refers to scrambled text that is visible to the naked eye or observer, but unintelligible without analysis. Steganography is writing that is not visible to the naked eye or observer, also known as *covered* or invisible writing.

The confusion could be from the English definition of *hidden*, which according to The Random House College Dictionary means "concealed, obscure, covert."[7] As a result, it's understandable why there have been misappropriations of definitions by people when describing cryptography and steganography. This English

---

[6] Cryptography Decrypted by H.X. Mel and Doris Baker, p. 24.
[7] Random House College Dictionary, 1979.

definition would imply an overlap between cryptography and steganography, which is simply not the case. When deciphering the differences between cryptography and steganography, ask yourself "is the message scrambled or invisible?" If it's scrambled it's cryptography, if it's invisible it's steganography.

Cardano's Grille

Italian (actually Milanese) Girolamo Cardano is credited with creating the first known grille cipher. It involves using a stiff sheet of paper, metal, or otherwise, with windows cut into random, yet planned, locations of the sheet. This sheet is known as a grill. An otherwise visibly normal message would actually have strategically placed letters that within itself make up another message, hidden within the visible message. The example in Figure 1.10 at first glance appears as a normal message.

T	H	E		W	E	A	T	H	E	R		H	A	S
B	E	E	N		V	E	R	Y		C	O	O	L	
L	A	T	E	L	Y	.		P	E	R	H	A	P	S
	T	H	E		F	A	L	L		W	I	L	L	
S	T	A	R	T		S	O	O	N	E	R		T	H
I	S		Y	E	A	R	.		P	R	A	C	T	I
C	A	L	L	Y		E	V	E	R	Y		M	A	P
L	E		H	A	S		S	T	A	R	T	E	D	
T	O		C	H	A	N	G	E		C	O	L	O	R
.		W	E		H	A	V	E		F	I	N	I	S
H	E	D		O	U	R		L	A	S	T		H	A
R	V	E	S	T		O	F		T	H	E		Y	E
A	R	.												

FIGURE 1.10 Cardano Grille with Hidden Message

But if the intended recipient knew to look for a hidden message contained with the normal message, he could use his Cardano Grill to identify the relevant letters that makeup the hidden message. By taking the sheet or grill with strategic holes cutout, he could lay the sheet over top of the message to reveal the hidden message. In this case the message reveals that "Troops arrive Monday" as illustrated in Figure 1.11.

The Cardano Grille cipher is still used today. For example, the Spam Mimic website uses this technique. But rather than use a grille to reveal the message, a program performs the hiding (encoding) as well as the decoding (Figure 1.12).

The goal here is to create what appears to be a spam message, but is actually a message encoded within another message. People receive countless spam messages every day. Unless some knew that a particular spam message contained

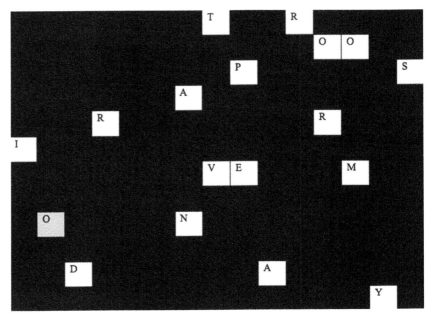

FIGURE 1.11 Cardano Grille with Overlay Revealing Hidden Message

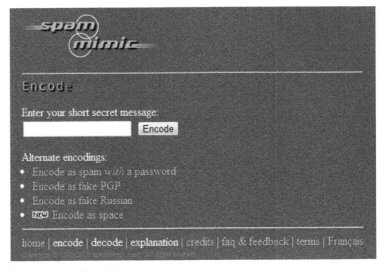

FIGURE 1.12 Spam Mimic Encoding

an encoded message, they would simply pass it off as another spam message. But intended recipient though could go to the Spam Mimic site, input their message, and decode the hidden message.

Invisible Ink

One of the first written accounts of secret ink dates back to the first century A.D. where Pliny the Elder wrote about his discovery that the milk of the tithymalus plant (a type of cactus) could be used for invisible writing.[8] This is noted as one of the first accounts of science around hiding the existence of a message (steganography).

Probably one of the most common forms of invisible ink is lemon juice. It can be used to write a message on a piece of paper, and when it dries it's invisible to the naked eye. But put the paper to warm source such as a light bulb, and the message will slowly appear. Many other acid based substances will oxidize and reveal themselves when exposed to heat include; urine, vinegar, wine, onion juice, milk, and even rain water combined with sulfuric acid.

Samuel Rubin's 1987 book, "The Secret Science of Covert Inks"[9] is probably the most comprehensive book on the subject. It details supposedly secret CIA invisible ink techniques which have been largely disclosed by the non-profit organization known as the "James Madison Project." For a list of these recipes, see the James Madison Project website http://www.jamesmadisonproject.org. It should be noted that the specific government agencies believe that some of these "formulas must remain hidden from the public,"[10] which is why they're not reproduced in this book.

Microdots

It's difficult to approach the subject of steganography without discussing microdots. It's mentioned in practically every book that discusses steganography or secret writing. It involves shrinking a photograph to the size of a period on a typed page. The dot could be a period, or a dot in a dotted "i", or hidden in a variety of other ways on the page.

Although the idea of microphotographs dates back to Paris in 1870, the F.B.I. got a tip from a double agent in 1940 that the Germans had perfected the technique to create a microdot.[11] It took them until 1941 to detect their first microdot on an envelope intercepted from a suspected German agent. Soon after, tiny strips of film were discovered under stamps. It was later discovered that the technology was being used for espionage. A variety of stolen information was discovered including uranium design information, production statistics, building plans, schematics, etc. At the time, the small Minox Camera was commonly used by spies to take pictures of documents (see Figure 1.13).

---

[8] The Puzzle Palace by James Branford, pp. 503–504.
[9] Samuel Rubin's 1987 book "The Secret Science of Covert Inks."
[10] http://www.jamesmadisonproject.org/ocdpage.html.
[11] The Code-Breakers by David Kahn, p. 525.

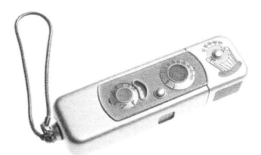

FIGURE 1.13 Minox "Spy" Camera.[12]

The process of creating the microdot involved take the thumbnail sized print from the camera and photographing again through a reverse microscope. This would shrink it to a diameter of 0.05 inches. It was then developed and a hypodermic needle was used to lift the dot and drop it over a period in a typed letter. The dot was then affixed in place using collodion (a common photography chemical).[13] Various magnification tools could be used by the recipient to view the contents of the microdot.

The only problem with using microdots was that the special ink they were written with was very shiny; a letter suspected of containing microdots could be held up to a light and viewed at eye-level, looking across the page. Held in a certain way, the microdot ink would shine while normal ink would not.

Although the specific inventor of microdot steganography is unknown, it is commonly credited to someone named Professor Zapp, inventor of the Minox subminiature camera. Thus, World War II microdot kits were often called Zapp outfits by British intelligence.

It also is important to note that microdot technology is more useful for sending an entire document, versus invisible ink which is more useful for sending a short message. The microdot could be used for documents that included diagrams & drawings, something invisible ink was just not capable of. Microdots are commonly used today by casinos for marking chips as well as automobile manufacturers for marking the authenticity of cars.

Printer Tracking Dots

Back in 2004, PCWorld[14] published an article raising awareness that printer manufacturers were printing hidden yellow dots to every page printed.

---

[12] CIA Minox Camera—http://www.flickr.com/photos/ciagov/5416180501/in/photostream.

[13] The Puzzle Palace by James Branford, p. 503–504.

[14] Government uses color laser printer technology to track documents—http://www.pcworld.com/article/118664/government_uses_color_laser_printer_technology_to_track_documents.html.

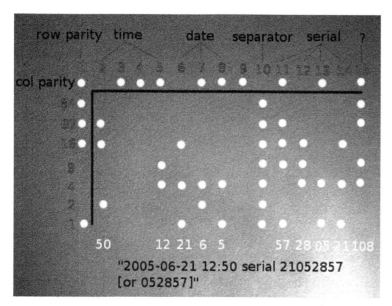

FIGURE 1.14 Printer Tracking Dots

The Electronic Frontier Foundation (EFF) picked up the story and cracked the codes for the DocuColor (Xerox) printers. EFF discovered that the yellow dots represented the serial number for the printer, as well as the time and date the document was printed. Interestingly enough, the dots are not visible to the naked eye. But with blue light and magnification, one can reveal the hidden dots (see Figure 1.14). The EFF then deciphered the grid to reveal the cipher behind the dots shown in Figure 1.15.

	1	2	3	4	5	6	7	8	9	10	11	12	13	14	15
col parity															
64															
32															
16															
8															
4															
2															
1															

[Clear] [Submit]

FIGURE 1.15 EFF DocuColor Dots Deciphering Program

It is strongly believed that these were designed for law enforcement forensics purposes. The EFF maintains a list of printers known to print these dots. The list can be found here, http://www.eff.org/pages/list-printers-which-do-or-do-not-display-tracking-dots. And if your printer is not listed, you can take your own printed page and use their online decoder to decipher the dots (Figure 1.15).

Watermarks

Watermarking is a technique with similarities to steganography. It has been around for centuries and is commonly used in money and stamps to assist in identifying counterfeiting. The idea behind watermarking is to create a translucent image on the paper to provide authenticity. Since mailing letters was far more expensive centuries back, it was common for people to use counterfeit stamps on their mail. For example, a translucent elephant watermark was used on stamps in India to deter counterfeiting.

Various watermarks are also added to money at the time of manufacture. For example, many denominations of paper money in the United States contain a watermark of the individual printed on the money. For example, on the $100 dollar bill, you will find a watermark of Benjamin Franklin if you illuminate the bill from behind (see Figure 1.16).

Digital watermarking is used to maintain ownership and authenticity of digital media such as music and videos.

It is important to note that although watermarking has many similarities to steganography in terms of embedding data, but the intent of watermarking is not to make it difficult to detect that embedded data, but rather make it difficult to remove the embedded data so as to prevent the unauthorized reuse of the file.

FIGURE 1.16 $100 Bill Translucent Watermark

SUMMARY

Secret communications encompass an interesting history throughout civilizations, wars, and cultures. Many of the highlighted cryptographic and steganographic secret communication methods are replicated in digital form today. Join us in this journey of digital data hiding as we explore many of the latest data hiding techniques across operating systems, mobile devices, multimedia, and other digital formats.

References

Branford, J. (1983a). *Invisible Ink. The puzzle palace* (1st ed., pp. 503–504). Brandford Books (September 29).

Branford, J. (1983b). *Collodion. The puzzle palace* (1st ed., pp. 503–504). Branford Books (September 29).

CIA – Minox Camera. <http://www.flickr.com/photos/ciagov/5416180501/in/photostream>.

CIAPhoto Stream – German Microdot. <http://www.flickr.com/photos/ciagov/with/5416242829/#photo_5416242829>.

Cisco password decrypter. <http://www.hope.co.nz/projects/tools/ciscopw.php>.

Fratini, S. (2002). Cardano's Grille. Encryption using a variant of the turning-grille method. *Mathematics Magazine*, 75(5), 389–396. 398. Article Stable URL: <http://www.jstor.org/stable/3219071>.

Government uses color laser printer technology to track documents. <http://www.pcworld.com/article/118664/government_uses_color_laser_printer_technology_to_track_documents.html>.

James Madison Project. <http://www.jamesmadisonproject.org>.

Johnny quest ring. Stephen A. Kallis, Jr. & Metro Washington Old Time Radio Club.

Kahn, D. (1967). *Microdot. The codebreakers* (p. 525). Scribner (revised and updated, 1996).

Luciano, D., & Prichett, G. (1987). Caesar cipher. Cryptology: From Caesar ciphers to public-key cryptosystems. *The College Mathematics Journal*, 18(1), 2–4. Article Stable URL: <http://wwww.maa.org/pubs/Calc_articles/ma079.pdf>.

Mel, H. X., & Baker, D. (2000). *DES. Cryptography decrypted* (1st ed., p. 24). Addison-Wesley Professional (December 31).

Microdot Mark IV camera. <https://www.cia.gov/cia/information/artifacts/markiv.jpg>.

Samuel Rubin's 1987 book "The Secret Science of Covert Inks". Breakout Publications, January 1987.

Singh, S. (1999). *The code book.* Anchor Books, A Division of Random House, Inc.. (p. 78).

Gualtieri, D. M. Spartan Scytale. <http://www.devgualtieri.com/>.

Fields, B. T. (1979). Vigenere cipher photo. Public domain (original author). Random House Dictionary.

This page is intentionally left blank

## CHAPTER 2

Four Easy Data Hiding Exercises

INFORMATION IN THIS CHAPTER:

- Hiding Data in Microsoft Word
- Image Metadata
- Mobile Device Data Hiding
- File Compression Tool Data Hiding

CONTENTS

[1]Much of the software we use on a daily basis contain feature that allow one to hide data. For example, in Microsoft Word a user can edit the Properties to insert an Author Name, Company, keywords, tag, and a variety of other data. This is commonly referred to as *metadata*. If the document is then sent to another user, that user may also edit the document. As this process occurs, Microsoft Word will track the ownership of the document, date of creation, change control, etc. This is additional metadata that is automatically added to the document. Many times these documents are then sent outside of the organization or posted on a website. This presents a security concern because information about individuals and the company are now inadvertently exposed to individuals outside of the organization. Would you be concerned if your name, company, phone number, Email address, and perhaps other sensitive information were exposed to anyone on the Internet?

The US Government is concerned about such exposures and has published multiple processes and procedures for properly cleansing documents of

---

[1] Understanding Metadata. http://www.niso.org/publications/press/Understanding Metadata.pdf.

Data Hiding http://dx.doi.org/10.1016/B978-1-59-749743-5.00002-X

metadata before publishing them. For example, the NSA published "Hidden Data and Metadata in Adobe PDF Files: Publication Risks and Countermeasures.[2]" It outlines procedures for sanitizing PDFs before posting to websites or sending to other organizations. This includes not only metadata, but also hidden layers used for engineering documents, obscured text and images, etc.

At Defcon 17 and 18, the guys from Informatica64 presented their tool called FOCA (Fingerprinting Organizations and Collected Archives).[3] The tool allows you to scan websites and online services to look for files and documents that contain interesting data such as metadata. The presentation exposed the enormous amount of information that is leaked by posting Word documents, Adobe PDFs, as well as web pages that comprise numerous websites. Many publishing tools allow the user to insert an Author, Reviewers, Company name, Company details, title, tags, etc. All of this information can be harvested using tools like FOCA to perform reconnaissance on target companies and government entities. Many organizations are unknowingly leaking this data to anyone on the Internet.

In this chapter we'll explore some common programs that allow data to be easily hidden from the casual viewer.

HIDING DATA IN MICROSOFT WORD

Microsoft Word remains the predominant word processor standard. In fact, many people using a Mac also use Microsoft Word as their word processor. Therefore it serves us well to begin our exploration by investigating the many ways in which data can be hidden within your standard Microsoft Word document.

Microsoft Word, Excel, and PowerPoint 2007 and 2010 provide a variety of ways to hide data within the document. These include comments, personal information, watermarks, invisible content, hidden content, and custom XML data. Using the Hidden Text font options provides an easy yet amazingly effective way to hide data. First, type a standard document, and additionally input the data you'd like to hide (see Figure 2.1).

---

[2] NSA "Hidden Data and Metadata in Adobe PDF Files: Publication Risks and Countermeasure" http://www.nsa.gov/ia/_files/app/pdf_risks.pdf.
[3] FOCADefCon17.http://www.slideshare.net/chemai64/defcon-17-tactical-fingerprinting-using-foca.

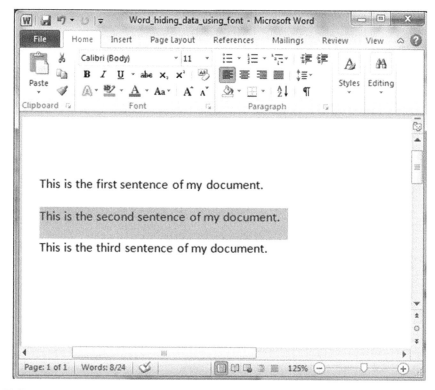

FIGURE 2.1 Inputting Data into a Microsoft Word Document to be Hidden

Then highlight the content you'd like to hide, and right-click and choose Font. You will notice in newer version of Microsoft Word a new checkbox labeled "Hidden." By selecting Hidden and then Save, you will notice that the highlighted text will be hidden from normal viewing (see Figures 2.2 and 2.3).

By default, hidden text is also not printed when printing the document. In order for an average user to know if there is hidden text they would need to go to File, Options, and select Display. Selecting the "Hidden Text" checkbox will enable formatting marks to alert a user to hidden text, and "Print Hidden Text" to determine if there is any hidden text (see Figure 2.4).

Another way to identify hidden text is to use the Inspect Document option in File => Info => Check for Issues => Inspect Document. The Inspect Document is actually a great way to identify a variety of metadata hidden within the document such as authors, comments, and possibly other personal identifiable information (PII). In addition it can be used to identify hidden text (see Figure 2.5).

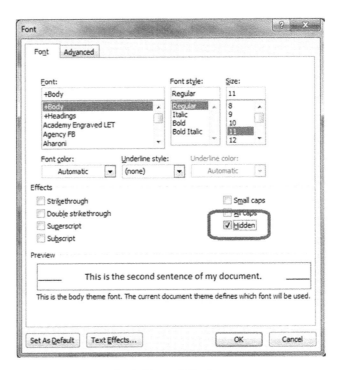

FIGURE 2.2 Using the Hidden Option in Microsoft Word

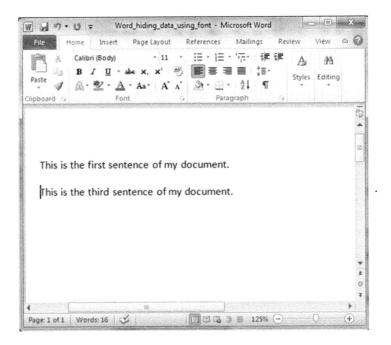

FIGURE 2.3 Microsoft Word Document after Hiding the Second Sentence

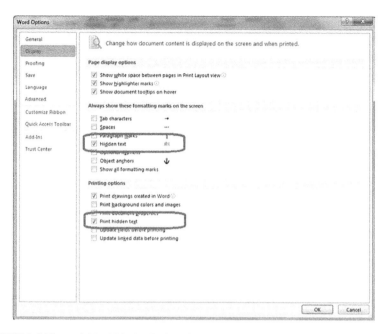

FIGURE 2.4 Microsoft Word Display Options for Identifying Hidden Text

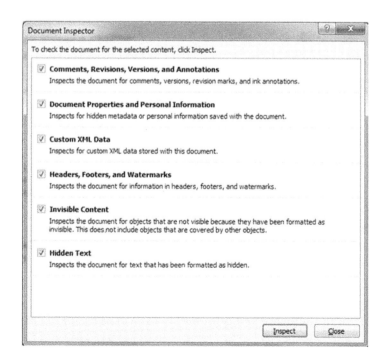

FIGURE 2.5 Using Document Inspector to Find Hidden Text and Other Metadata

Select Inspect to have the Document Inspector identify the metadata and create a report of results. In this example, the Document Inspector correctly identifies the Hidden Text and allows the user to remove it if they desire. The interesting thing here is that most people never check for the existence of Hidden Text and therefore have no idea it's there (see Figure 2.6).

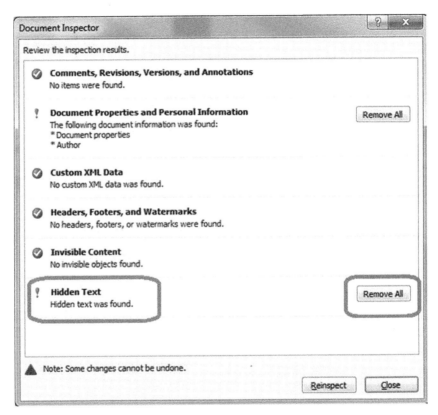

FIGURE 2.6 Document Inspector Identified Hidden Text in the Document

It is important to note that the only Hidden Text identified is text hidden using the Font dialog box. For example, if text is hidden from viewing using the white text on the white background, the Document Inspector will not identify this hidden text.

The ability to hide data in the document is practical if you want to print two versions of the same document, one with the hidden data and one without. This is common for PowerPoint presentations when an individual may print the slides for the audience and print the slides with notes for the presenter.

There are a variety of other things that can be hidden within Microsoft Word 2010 Properties section, including tags, author's name, comment, etc. (see Figure 2.7).

FIGURE 2.7 Microsoft Word Properties and Metadata

In addition, the Properties drop-down allows access to the Advanced Properties where customs fields may be added as well (see Figure 2.8).

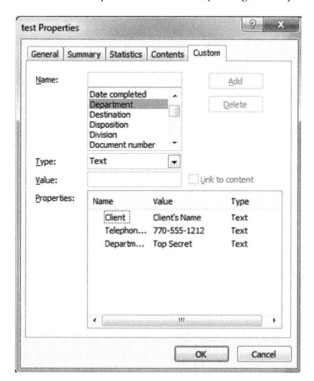

FIGURE 2.8 Custom Tab in Microsoft Word Advanced Properties

It's important to note that these are not displayed in the main Properties view, and therefore must be viewed by manually opening the Custom Tab in the Advanced Properties window.

IMAGE METADATA

Agencies such as the FBI and law enforcement use metadata to track and capture criminals. When criminals transmit pictures or post them to websites, the metadata stored in the picture can reveal a criminal's location and the device from which the picture was taken. The "BTK" killer (Dennis Rader) murdered more than a dozen people over a 30 year period while taunting local police and media with clues and evidence from the murders.[4] The key to linking the evidence to the serial killer stemmed from a floppy disk that was received. The digital forensic examiner analyzed the deleted data on the disk and found a deleted Microsoft Word file with metadata. This metadata indicated that the file was originally created on a computer at the nearby church and created by a person named Dennis. Coincidentally, this was also the church where Dennis Rader served as president of the church's congregation council! Further investigation linked other evidence, including DNA, to Dennis Rader eventually leading to a conviction of 10 life sentences.[5]

There are numerous tools for viewing and modifying metadata within pictures, especially JPEG formats. Since JPEG is the most common format used on mobile devices and cameras today, we'll focus on that for our analysis. EXIF stands for Exchangeable Image File Format and is a standard for many media formats including JPEG, TIFF, etc.[6] The format outlines tags or header formats for a file that can be used by cameras, scanners, and other products to embed metadata in the media file. These EXIF headers are also a way to hide data from casual viewers, and escape detection by many network security tools.

Google's Picasa is a free download available for multiple platforms including Windows and Mac. The image editing software allows the metadata within the EXIF header to be viewed and modified. When an image is opened for editing within Picasa, the Properties pane on the right allows you to view the EXIF header information. This may include Camera data, such as the type of Camera (or mobile device with camera), data/time the picture was taken, and other identifiable information. Some people choose to cleanse this data before posting it online or sharing it with others, as sometimes the picture

[4] Dennis Rader—Biography. http://www.biography.com/people/dennis-rader-241487?page=2.
[5] How Computer Forensics Solved the BTK Killer Case. http://precisioncomputerinvestigations. wordpress.com/2010/04/14/how-computer-forensics-solved-the-btk-killer-case/.
[6] Exif—MIT. http://www.media.mit.edu/pia/Research/deepview/exif.html.

may also include GPS location data revealing where the picture was taken. For privacy reasons, some users prefer to remove this hidden data (see Figure 2.9).

FIGURE 2.9 Viewing and Editing Properties and EXIF Headers in Google's Picasa

Picasa also allows you to edit the Caption (tag) in the photo, which is really another EXIF header data field. As mentioned earlier, this also makes for a simple location in which to hide data from casual viewers or security detection products. Simply click the Show/Hide Caption button to edit the Caption (see Figure 2.10).

FIGURE 2.10 Adding Caption to Photo and EXIF Header

Microsoft Windows 7 also provides an easy way to view and modify the EXIF header data or metadata within an image (see Figure 2.11).

FIGURE 2.11 Viewing Image Metadata in Windows 7

Also, by right-clicking on the image, you can modify the EXIF headers. In the following example, we can change the Camera maker from HTC to Motorola (see Figure 2.12).

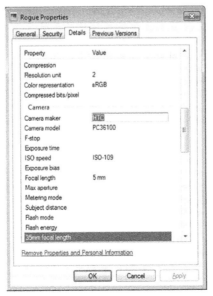
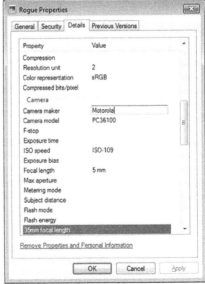

FIGURE 2.12 Changing the Camera Maker Metadata from HTC to Motorola

Although this may be a rudimentary way to hide data in a photograph, it's easy for most people to do, and as a result can be an efficient way to hide data and disseminate it to other individuals. Unknowing users also leave behind traces of their identity with pictures as well. Law enforcement commonly uses this metadata, especially GPS data to locate the whereabouts of an individual at the time the photo was taken, and from what device the photo was taken from.

MOBILE DEVICE DATA HIDING

The Google Android mobile platform, based on the Linux kernel, is supported across a wide range of devices. This proliferation has resulted in a plethora of applications written for the Android operating system. Specific security features have been built into the based platform from which the individual hardware manufacturers build from to create their own "flavor" of Android for their hardware. But there are a number of consistencies including the Dalvik virtual machines to create an application sandbox.[7]

Some data hiding applications allow the native Linux functionality to be leveraged for hiding data. The Hide it Pro application available from Google Play (Android Marketplace) provides a number of stealthy features to evade detection from the casual or nosey observer. Hide it Pro is designed to allow the user to hide files and folders from other users or the Android smartphone.

The application hides itself behind a faux application called "Audio Manager" also deployed during the install. By pressing the Audio Image for a few seconds, it will then bring up Hide it Pro. This provides a clever way to provide some security through obscurity (see Figure 2.13).

In addition, access to the application can be protected using a PIN or password, and is chosen the first time you run the application as a second layer of security before access is allowed to the application (see Figure 2.14).

Hide it Pro creates a separate directory for storing the files, and also renames the files with an arbitrary extension. This directory is found on the SD card under /mnt/sdcard in ProgramData/Android/Language. Normally, Linux directory names and file names created with a dot "." are hidden. Therefore, Hide it Pro uses this to further disguise itself on the SD card, by creating a hidden directory in this case ".fr" in the Language directory.

---

[7] Hoog, A. Android forensics (p. 87), Syngress Publishing.

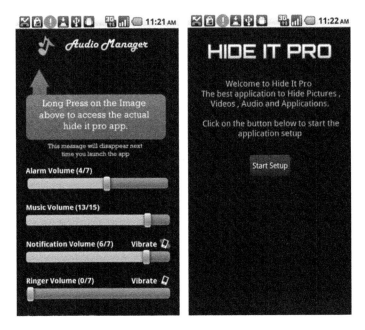

FIGURE 2.13 Hide it Pro

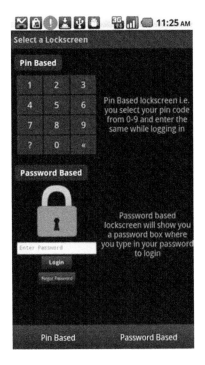

FIGURE 2.14 Hide it Pro PIN or Passcode Entry

This is intentional as Android Gallery ignores files with filenames that are prepended with a ".". Hide it Pro uses this technique to hide files from a casual user looking for multimedia files. When the install is complete, the user can hide multimedia files through Hide it Pro. Simply choose your file within your Android Gallery and select Menu and then Share. Audio Manager will appear in the menu along with Email, Messaging, Facebook, etc. (see Figure 2.15).

FIGURE 2.15 Viewing a Picture in Gallery and Sharing with Audio Manager

A file manager window will pop-up allowing you to create or select a folder and move the file to Audio Manager (Hide it Pro) (see Figure 2.16).

Files saved in Hide it Pro are renamed with a *.bin extension. A Linux directory listing reveals the aforementioned hidden directories and renamed files, as shown in Figure 2.17.

Once hidden within Hide it Pro, the multimedia files are removed from the Android Gallery. But of course the files can still be accessed through Hide it Pro

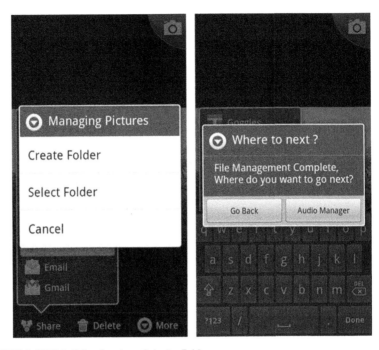

FIGURE 2.16 Hide it Pro Create or Select a Folder

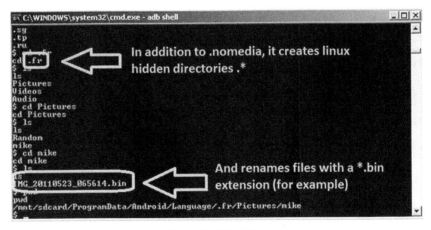

FIGURE 2.17 Directories and Files Created by Hide it Pro

by pressing and holding Audio Manager for 5 s, and entering your password into Hide it Pro (see Figure 2.18).

FIGURE 2.18 Accessing Your Hidden Files in Hide it Pro

FILE COMPRESSION TOOL DATA HIDING

WinRAR is one of many compression and archive utilities, similar to WinZip. WinRAR is supported on Linux, Mac OS, and Microsoft Windows (www.win-rar.com). One interesting feature is that it can self-heal a corrupt archive. This feature can also be circumvented to allow one to hide an archive within a carrier file. The recipient can then run the carrier file through WinRAR, allow it to self-heal or repair the archive, and reveal the hidden archive.

We begin by creating an archive that contains the data we want to hide. We start with a text file called "mike.txt" with our hidden message (see Figure 2.19).

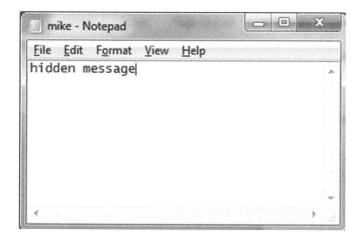

FIGURE 2.19 Hidden Message File

Next we create an archive called mike.rar archive with mike.txt within it. This involves downloading and installing WinRAR for your platform (Windows, Linux, Mac OS X, etc.) from the website at www.rarlab.com. When you start up WinRAR select Add to add our hidden message file (mike.txt) to create a new archive (see Figure 2.20).

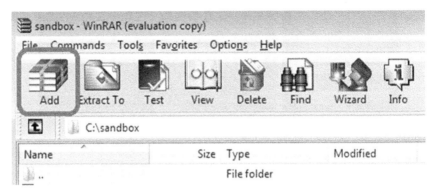

FIGURE 2.20 Run WinRAR and Click Add

Under the Files tab, and in the "Files to add" dialog box select our mike.txt file with the hidden message. And then select OK to create our mike.rar archive (see Figures 2.21 and 2.22).

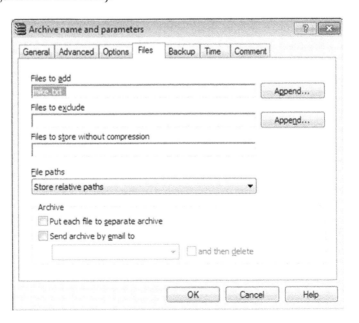

FIGURE 2.21 Add mike.txt to Archive and Click OK

FIGURE 2.22 mike.rar Archive Created

Next we hide the archive in a JPEG file. In this example, we choose an innocuous JPEG file "Class.JPG" as our carrier. Using the copy command in DOS, we add the /b option to treat the file as a binary file. Additionally we use the "+" symbol to combine two files. In this case we're combining our carrier file "Class.JPG" with the archive file we want to hide "mike.rar," and specify an output file "newimage.JPG."

```
c:\sandbox>copy /b class.jpg + mike.rar newimage.jpg
class.JPG
mike.rar
1 file(s) copied.
```

This technique allows you to actually append the WinRAR archive to the JPEG, beyond the EOF (End of File) marker. This approach allows the JPEG to appear normally in a viewer, as the viewer will normally ignore data beyond the EOF marker, make this a nice place to hide data.

```
C:\sandbox>dir
Directory of C:\sandbox
04/27/2012 11:43 AM <DIR> .
04/27/2012 11:43 AM <DIR> ..
03/10/2012 10:59 AM 4,940,676 class.JPG
03/21/2012 01:48 PM 89 mike.rar
03/21/2012 01:48 PM 17 mike.txt
03/21/2012 01:50 PM 4,940,765 newimage.jpg
```

We now have our hidden message, compressed in WinRAR, and hidden within a JPEG image. At this point it could be transmitted to our recipient. Next, let's review how the recipient can now extract and reveal the hidden message.

Upon receipt, the recipient takes the JPEG and renames it with a *.RAR extension as follows:

```
c:\sandbox>copy newimage.jpg newimage.rar
1 file(s) copied.
c:\sandbox>dir
Directory of C:\sandbox
04/27/2012 11:43 AM <DIR> .
04/27/2012 11:43 AM <DIR> ..
03/21/2012 01:50 PM 4,940,765 newimage.jpg
03/21/2012 01:50 PM 4,940,765 newimage.rar
```

WinRAR provides a Repair feature for repairing damaged archives. It can also be used to extract the hidden message. Within WinRAR we select "Repair Damaged Archive" and choose the newly created *.RAR file. WinRAR will detect that the JPEG carrier file has a RAR archive within it. Repair will repair the damaged archive and will extract the RAR archive from the JPEG (see Figure 2.23).

This will create a "rebuilt" RAR file and also alerts us that it contains a "mike. txt" within the rebuilt archive. This creates a file called "rebuilt.newimage.rar" (see Figure 2.24).

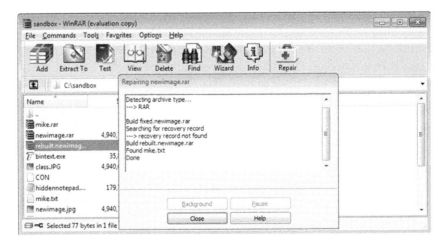

FIGURE 2.23 WinRAR Repairing the Archive

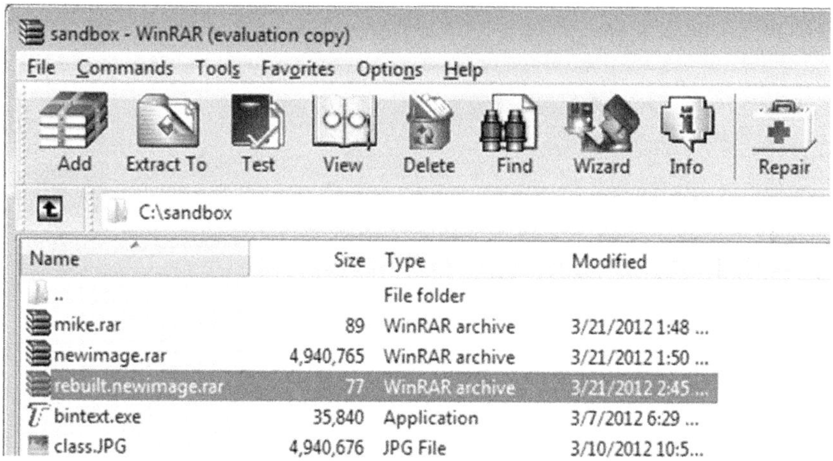

FIGURE 2.24 Rebuilt File *rebuilt.newimage.rar*

Using the "Extract To" option, the recipient can now extract the mike.txt file from the rebuilt WinRAR archive *rebuilt.newimage.rar,* thus allowing the recipient to reveal the hidden message (see Figure 2.25).

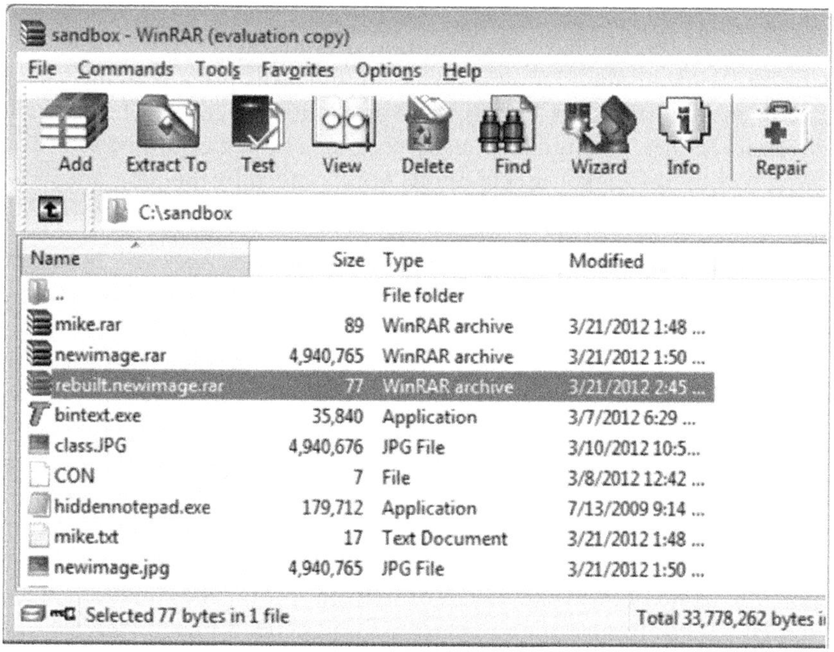

FIGURE 2.25 Using *Extract To* for Extracting the Archive and Revealing mike.txt

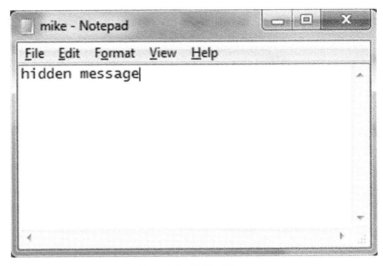

FIGURE 2.26 Opening mike.txt to Reveal the Hidden Message

We can now open mike.txt to reveal the original hidden message (see Figure 2.26).

SUMMARY

In this chapter we explored some common data hiding tools and techniques. Microsoft Word, Adobe PDF, and Image editing tools provide many ways to create or modify metadata in files, thus providing a plethora of options for hiding data in files. Additionally, many programs can be exploited to provide a covert way to hide data using methods not intended by the program, as was the case with WinRAR.

As we move toward examining "true" steganography we will investigate methods that will hide payloads under the cover of a digital carrier using sophisticated algorithms. For professional steganography to be effective, it must evade detection through the normal manner in which we use them. For example, viewing an original photograph side by side with the imposter must not reveal any defects that could be noticed even by a keen observer. For audio files, the original recording when played must be indistinguishable from that of the imposter. More sophisticated embedding algorithms will leave only subtle statistical traces or artifacts when examining the original versus imposter, which without the aid of the original would be nearly impossible to identify in the wild. For network protocols, variations would be difficult if not impossible to detect without generating an overwhelming number of false positives. We'll be performing deeper analysis of many of these techniques in the chapters that follow, but next let's review some steganography fundamentals.

References

Dennis Rader—Biography. <http://www.biography.com/people/dennis-rader-241487?page=2>.

Exif—MIT. <http://www.media.mit.edu/pia/Research/deepview/exif.html>.

FOCADefCon17.<http://www.slideshare.net/chemai64/defcon-17-tactical-fingerprinting-using-foca>.

Hoog, A. Android forensics (p. 87).

How Computer Forensics Solved the BTK Killer Case. <http://precisioncomputerinvestigations.wordpress.com/2010/04/14/how-computer-forensics-solved-the-btk-killer-case/>.

NSA "Hidden Data and Metadata in Adobe PDF Files: Publication Risks and Countermeasure" <http://www.nsa.gov/ia/_files/app/pdf_risks.pdf>.

Understanding Metadata. <http://www.niso.org/publications/press/UnderstandingMetadata.pdf>.

This page is intentionally left blank

## CHAPTER 3

Steganography

INFORMATION IN THIS CHAPTER:

- Introduction
- Steganographic Techniques
- Steganalysis

CONTENTS

INTRODUCTION

Operation Shady RAT was believed to be the largest corporate espionage attack ever, occurring from 2006 and continuing through 2011, and was targeted at stealing intellectual property from the most prominent government agencies and government contractors. The attackers used steganographic techniques to hide command and control messages in digital photographs and within website HTML pages. But how did the attack happen? And how were the files distributed? This requires a closer look at the analysis performed by McAfee and Symantec researchers, who combined, broke the story.[1]

Specific users at these agencies and government contractors were sent targeted E-mails containing attachments such as Microsoft Word or Excel documents, as well as Adobe PDF files. These files were titled with specially crafted names citing relevant information to that particular agency or contractor. These unsuspecting users then opened the file causing a Trojan to be dropped and installed onto their computer. These Trojans then reached out to URLs pointing to image or HTML files embedded with hidden commands.

Symantec determined that these images contained hidden commands that caused these infected computers to reach out to "Command & Control" servers on the Internet, thereby allowing information to be syphoned from

---

[1] Revealed: Operation Shady RAT McAfee—www.mcafee.com/us/resources/white.../wp-operation-shady-rat.pdf.

Data Hiding. http://dx.doi.org/10.1016/B978-1-59-749743-5.00003-1

these computers. Symantec also determined that the commands were hidden in the files using steganographic techniques.[2] Since most firewalls and web application filters allow images and HTML to pass, the files were transported back to the user undetected.

Attackers are becoming more sophisticated about how they use steganography. Historically, digital steganography has been used for covert communications and hiding sensitive data. The following diagram highlights some key events during the digital steganography era: (see Figure 3.1)

Advancements in digital steganography

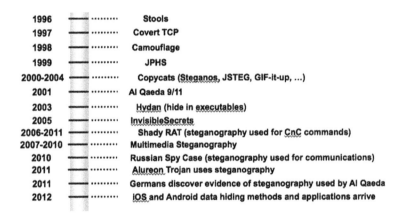

1996	Stools
1997	Covert TCP
1998	Camouflage
1999	JPHS
2000-2004	Copycats (Steganos, JSTEG, GIF-it-up, ...)
2001	Al Qaeda 9/11
2003	Hydan (hide in executables)
2005	InvisibleSecrets
2006-2011	Shady RAT (steganography used for CnC commands)
2007-2010	Multimedia Steganography
2010	Russian Spy Case (steganography used for communications)
2011	Alureon Trojan uses steganography
2011	Germans discover evidence of steganography used by Al Qaeda
2012	iOS and Android data hiding methods and applications arrive

FIGURE 3.1 Advancements in Digital Steganography

Over the past five years there has been an increase in steganographic techniques in malware. This approach allows malware attackers to distribute malicious software through firewalls, web application filters, intrusion prevention systems, and other layers of defense without being detected. Let's take a look at the fundamental approaches to hiding data in carrier files such as digital images, HTML pages, and other common file types.

STEGANOGRAPHIC TECHNIQUES

As outlined in Chapter 1, steganography is covered or invisible writing. In digital steganography, the user typically uses a program to hide a message or file within a carrier file, then sends that carrier file to the recipient or posts it on a site for

---

[2] The Truth Behind the Shady RAT—Symantec—http://www.symantec.com/connect/blogs/truth-behind-shady-rat.

download. Then the recipient receives the file and uses the same program to reveal the hidden message or file. For further protection, some hiding programs may also password protect the hidden message while other data hiding programs may encrypt and password protect the hidden contents.

There are various techniques and methods for hiding digital data divided into two main categories:

> *Insertion:* Insertion involves inserting additional content. This content may include the hidden message, as well as file markers as identifiers to the steganography program indicating the location of the hidden payload. Insertion usually takes advantage of unused space within the file format.
> *Substitution:* Substitution involves changing or swapping the existing bytes such that nothing new is inserted into the carrier file, but rather existing bytes are tweaked or changed to make them unnoticeable visibly or audibly. One such example is Least Significant Bit (LSB) substitution, whereby the steganography program modifies the Least Significant Bit of a series of bytes in the file, by changing those bits from a 0 to a 1, or a 1 to a 0.

Insertion Methods

In a way, insertion could be considered a form of modification, but for the purposes of steganography, it's important to distinguish the two. In steganography, it is important to think in terms of the existing data or virgin carrier file. With insertion, the existing data is not changed, but rather additional data is added to the file. In modification, the existing data is changed without the addition of additional data. In terms of the overall file, in both cases the file has been modified, but in terms of the data, insertion adds data, whereas modification changes the existing data. But as we will soon discover, many steganography programs use a combination of both.

Append Insertion

Appending data to the end of a file is probably one of the most common and simplest forms of digital steganography. Many file types allow data to be appended to them, without any corruption of the file. The following file is an unmodified JPEG file viewed in WinHex (Figure 3.2). WinHex is a hexadecimal (hex) editor. It allows files to be viewed in their raw form, but unlike a text editor, all of the data is displayed including carriage-return characters and executable code. All data is displayed in its two-digit hexadecimal notation. This is displayed in the middle column. The left-hand column is the counter or offset allowing you to track the location within the file. The right-hand column displays the data in ASCII format. Due to the limitations of ASCII, not all data has an ASCII representation.

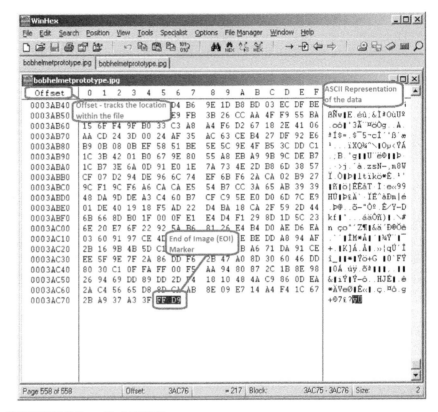

FIGURE 3.2 Unmodified JPEG File

A normal JPEG file has an End of Image (EOI) marker as indicated by 0xFF 0xD9. We can scroll to the end of the file to validate this EOI marker as demonstrated in Figure 3.2.

In the next file, the steganography program JPEGX[3] was used to hide data. We can open the newly modified file in WinHex to view the data appended to the end of the file as shown in Figure 3.3. Note that this data immediately follows the EOI marker 0xFF 0xD9.

Typically data hidden beyond the EOI marker is typically ignored when viewing the file, but usually an indication of a modified file with hidden data.

Prepend Insertion
Any type of file that provides comment fields provides the opportunity for inserting content without any effect to the visual image. For example, HTML files and JPEGs are particularly vulnerable to these techniques. In the case of

---

[3] JPEGX http://www.nerdlogic.org.

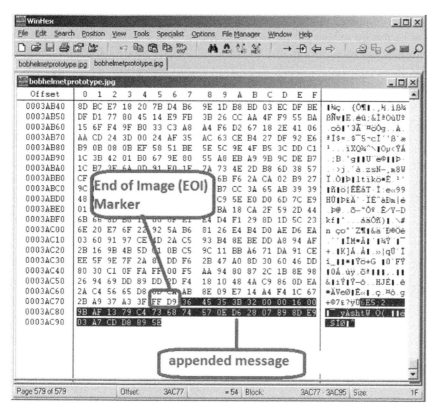

FIGURE 3.3 JPEG File with Appended Data

JPEGs, up to 65,533 bytes of comment data can be inserted into the file, which is invisible when the JPEG is viewed.[4]

JPEG files are partitioned with file markers, with each marker represented by a 0xFF. These have specific relevance to the image layout, format, and other details as shown in Table 3.1.

Table 3.1 JFIF (JPEG File Image Format)

Marker	Value (Hex)	Size (bytes)	Details
SOI	FF D8	2	Start of Image
APP0	FF E0	2	App Marker (file details)
SOF0	FF C0	2	Start of Frame (width, height, etc.)
SOS	FF DA	2	Start of Scan (image itself)
EOI	FF D9	2	End of Image/End of File (EOF)

[4] http://www.findarticles.com/p/articles/mi_zdpcm/is_200409/ai_n7184572/pg_2.

With all of the data fields available in the JPEG file format available at the beginning of the file, there are numerous areas in which hide data. The following demonstrates an unmodified file compared to one modified using JPHideand-Seek[5] (See Figure 3.4). Notice the insertion and modification of the data between the JPEG App marker 0xFF 0xE0 and Start of Frame marker 0xFF 0xC0.

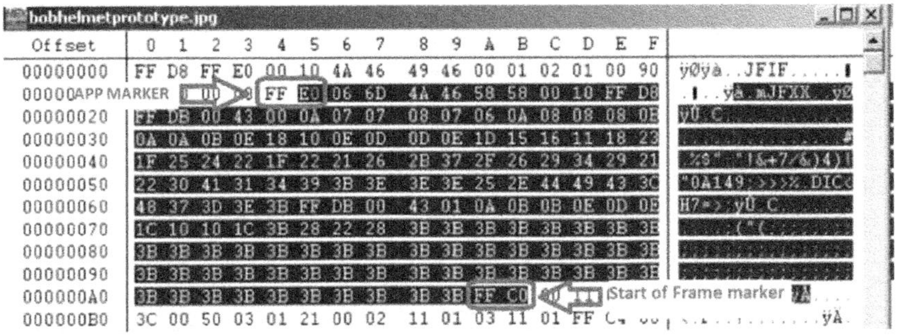

FIGURE 3.4 Prepending Data to a JPEG File

The comment fields in JPEGs allow numerous data to be hidden with minimal sophistication. Although the comment field in a JPEG could allow up to 65,533 bytes of comment data, it must be at least a minimum of 2 bytes. In the case of the APP0 marker, any metadata not recognized by the Decoder (viewing program) are skipped, making this a perfect location for hiding data.

Modification

The most common form of steganographic modification involves modifying the Least Significant Bit (LSB) of one or more bytes within a file. Essentially the bit is changed from a 0 to a 1, or a 1 to a 0. It renders the resulting modified file. These bits when reassembled reveal the original hidden message. It is almost impossible for a human to detect the modifications visually or audibly.

LSB

I find when teaching students that they struggle with understanding the LSB modification technique. I think the reason is that many books describe the concept accurately, but unfortunately in a very technical way that many students find hard to understand. Let's start with the basics.

For example, Least Significant Bit (LSB) modification takes advantage of 24-bit color palettes. In a 24-bit color palette you have three representations; Red, Green, and Blue (RGB). This is similar to the video representation in

---

[5] Latham. A. JPHideandSeek. http://linux01.gwdg.de/~alatham/stego.html.

component video with your television, where you have a Red, Green, and Blue cable delivering the video signal to your television.

In an image's 24-bit color palette, 8-bits are assigned to each of the three colors, essentially providing 256 shades of Red, 256 shades of Green, and 256 shades of Blue, as represented in Figure 3.5.

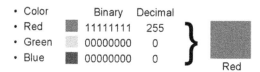

FIGURE 3.5 24-Bit Color Palette

Since our eyes can only interpret Red, Green, and Blue, it is the combination of these three colors that provides the color for each pixel that makes up the 24-bit image. Viewing the contents of an image, you will have three hexadecimal numbers (triplets) that represent the Red, Green, and Blue.

In LSB modification, the last bit (or least significant bit) of each 8-bit color representation is modified from a 0 to 1, or 1 to 0, or is unchanged (Figure 3.6).

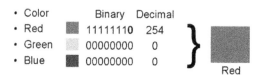

FIGURE 3.6 Modification of LSB

Each of these individual LSBs combined represent the inserted content. In the case of a text message, the LSBs are recombined to create the 8-bit representation of an ASCII character (Figure 3.7).

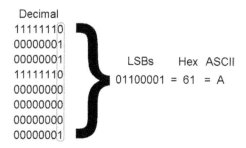

FIGURE 3.7 Least Significant Bit Example

It provides a method of hiding that is virtually undetectable through normal visual means, making it a respectable covert method. Usually only through statistical analysis can it be detected in its standalone form. The example in Figure 3.8 compares the colors created from Figure 3.5 and Figure 3.6. The difference between the original and the LSB modified is practically invisible to the naked eye.

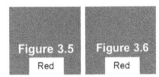

FIGURE 3.8 Comparing the Two Colors Before and After LSB Modification

The following example (Figure 3.9) shows before and after images. It's virtually impossible for the human eye to detect differences between the two files.

FIGURE 3.9 Comparison of Original File and File With Modified LSBs

Distributing these Least Significant Bits throughout a file provides a covert method of storing a message, while possibly not even changing the size of the file! File comparisons between the original file and the modified file can detect the modification, but that's assuming you have the original virgin file.

This type of modification works on 24-bit image files such as JPEGs and 24-bit BMP files. These types of files (RGB) are also called "True Color" file formats. LSB modification also works with 8-bit BMP images files as well, as is the case with ImageHide. Common programs that use this type of hiding technique include:

- S-Tools.
- ImageHide.
- Steganos.

Hiding in PDFs (Insertion Meets LSB)

wbStego4open[6](http://wbstego.wbailer.com) is a steganography open source tool supported on Windows and Linux platforms. wbStego4open allows files to be hidden in BMP, TXT, HTM, and PDF files without an visually detectable changes. You can also create a so-called Copyright file that can be embedded and hidden in the file as well. There are very few steganography programs that allow a user to hide data in PDFs. We begin by kicking off the program and choosing our PDF file (Figure 3.10).

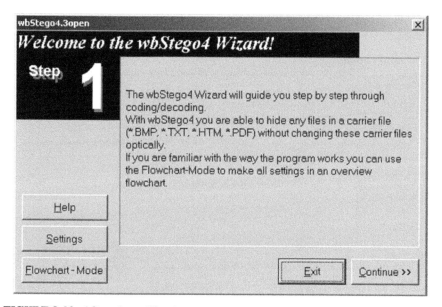

FIGURE 3.10 wbStego4open Wizard

The program takes advantage of the PDF headers to add additional information that is irrelevant when the PDF is viewed in the Adobe Acrobat Reader (Figure 3.11). In addition, when wbStego inserts data (in this case copyright non-encrypted data), it leverages both insertion and LSB methods.

It starts by converting each ASCII character of the insertion data to its binary form. Then wbStego4open represents each binary digit as a hexadecimal 20 or 09, with 20 representing a binary 0, and 09 representing a binary 1. For example, within the wbStego4open Copyright Manager we entered an address that included the word "Oblivion." wbStego4open converts the ASCII characters to their binary equivalents, and represents each binary digit as a 0x20 or 0x09 as shown in Figure 3.12.

---

[6] wbStego4open—http://wbstego.wbailer.com.

FIGURE 3.11 Inserting Copyright Info Using wbStego4open

ASCII	Binary	Hex
O	01001111	20 09 20 20 09 09 09 09
b	01100010	20 09 09 20 20 20 09 20
l	01101100	20 09 09 20 09 09 20 20
i =	01101001 =	20 09 09 20 09 20 20 09
v	01110110	20 09 09 09 20 09 09 20
i	01101001	20 09 09 20 09 20 20 09
o	01101111	20 09 09 20 09 09 09 09
n	01101110	20 09 09 20 09 09 09 20

FIGURE 3.12 wbStego4open Conversion

All of these hexadecimal equivalents are then embedded into the PDF file. Scanning the contents of a file modified by wbStego4open we reveal a file riddled with octets consisting or 20s and 09s (Figure 3.13).

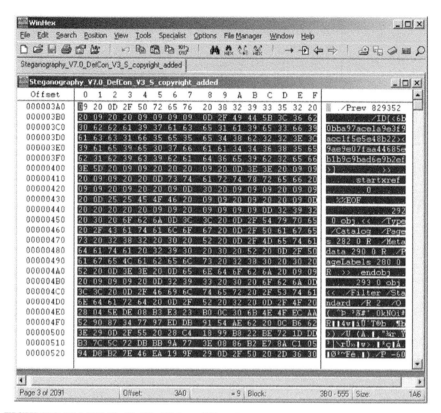

FIGURE 3.13 A PDF File Modified Using wbStego4open

Taking each of the octets and extracting their LSBs, the LSBs can then be combined to identify the ASCII character in binary representation. Converting the binary back to ASCII reveals the original message contents.

wbStego4open certainly supports files not commonly supported by other programs, in this case Adobe PDFs. In fact, the previous example was actually performed on a password-protected Adobe PDF file. Note that although it was password protected, we were still allowed to modify the PDF. Arguably this is not considered a vulnerability, but it does reveal the need for stronger protection, such as signing the PDF with a digital signature, thus notifying the receiver that the file has been modified. Password-protected Adobe PDF files protect primarily against printing and/or copying content. A digital certificate would protect against content modification. It would allow content to be modified, but would alert the receiver that the document has been modified, and therefore should not be trusted (Figure 3.14).

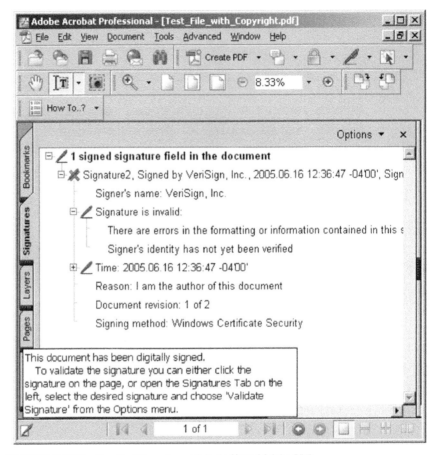

FIGURE 3.14 The Result of Changing a Digitally Signed Adobe PDF

Hiding in Executables (Hydan)

Hydan (http://www.crazyboy.com/hydan)[7] is a tool that allows data to be hidden in an executable. It is written by Rakan El-Khalil who has presented at many conferences including CodeCon and BlackHat. Hydan uses reverse engineering of binary code to determine the best places to hide data in the executable. To perform this it leverages Mammon's libdisasm, an x86 disassembly library. Binaries allow very little room for hiding data. Where the ration may be one byte of hidden data for every 17 bytes in a JPEG image, an executable may only allow one byte for every 150 bytes of code. Of course, it's a careful procedure of modifying the file so as to not break the host executable file.

Hydan runs under many flavors of Linux and FreeBSD. In this example, we use the "tar" binary to hide a message:

---

[7] Rakan, E-K. Hydan—http://www.crazyboy.com/hydan.

```
[root@localhost hydan]# ls -al
total 2760
drwx------   5 1000      users       4096 Jun   9 17:42 .
drwxr-xr-x   3 root      root        4096 Jun   9 17:42 ..
-rw-r--r--   1 root      root           7 Jun   9 17:36 message.txt
-rwxr-xr-x   1 root      root      150252 Jun   9 16:40 tar
[root@localhost hydan]# ./hydan tar message.txt > tar.steg
Password:
Done. Embedded 16/16 bytes out of a total possible 561 bytes.
Encoding rate: 1/201
[root@localhost hydan]# ls -al
total 2760
drwx------   5 1000      users       4096 Jun   9 17:42 .
drwxr-xr-x   3 root      root        4096 Jun   9 17:42 ..
-rw-r--r--   1 root      root           7 Jun   9 17:36 message.txt
-rwxr-xr-x   1 root      root      150252 Jun   9 16:40 tar
-rwxr-xr-x   1 root      root      150252 Jun   9 17:43 tar.steg
[root@localhost hydan]# ./hydan-decode tar.steg
Password:
hideme
[root@localhost hydan]# ./tar.steg -xvf hydan-0.13.tar
hydan/
hydan/CVS/
hydan/CVS/Root
hydan/CVS/Repository
hydan/CVS/Entries
hydan/msg
hydan/TODO
hydan/Makefile
.
.
.
```

As you can see, a new "tar" binary (tar.steg) is created. Testing it's functionality with the hidden data, it operates exactly the same as the legitimate tar binary. Rakan's tool demonstrates not only the effectiveness of hiding data in an executable, but how easy it really is. In addition, the tool can be used for attaching digital signatures, embedding watermarks, and modifying malware to evade antivirus detection.

Hydan may sometimes introduce executable runtime errors so it's not fool-proof, but it does work fairly well. Hydan is not as efficient as other techniques used for hiding content in images or sound files. There is less opportunity and therefore less room for hiding content in executables, so the ratio of available bytes is far less than that of image files. Nonetheless it's a unique method of data hiding that could be overlooked by the casual or well-trained investigator. It is also important to note that many steganalysis programs (open source and commercial) fail to look at executables altogether.

Hiding in HTML

Snow (www.darkside.com.au/snow/)[8] is a program written by Matthew Kwan to allow data to be hidden in ASCII text at the end of lines by using tabs and spaces which are not visible when viewed in viewers. The program allows the use of ICE (Information Concealment Engine) encryption. It was originally written for DOS and the program is now open source.

As stated in the man page,[9] "the data is concealed in the text file by appending sequences of up to seven spaces, interspersed with tabs. This usually allows 3 bits to be stored every eight columns."

```
OPTIONS
     -C Compress the data if concealing, or uncompress it if
     extracting.
     -Q Quiet mode. If not set, the program reports statistics
     such as compression percentages and amount of available
     storage space used.
     -S Report on the approximate amount of space available for
     hidden message in the text file. Line length is taken
     into account, but other options are ignored.
     -p password
     If this is set, the data will be encrypted with this
     password during concealment, or decrypted during
     extraction.
     -l line-len
     When appending whitespace, snow will always produce
     lines shorter than this value. By default it is set to 80.
     -f message-file
     The contents of this file will be concealed in the
     Input text file.
```

[8] Snow—www.darkside.com.au/snow/.
[9] Snow man page—http://www.darkside.com.au/snow/manual.html.

```
-m message-string
The contents of this string will be concealed in the
input text file. Note that, unless a newline is
somehow included in the string, a newline will not be
printed when the message is extracted.
```

The tool is run from the command line:

```
C:\>snow.exe -C -m "aaaaaaaaaaaaaaaa" -p "zzzzzzzz" SpyHunter.htm
    SpyHunterwithsnow.htm
Compressed by 50.00%
Message used approximately 4.18% of available space.
```

Comparing the original HTML file and the file with the hidden content, we see no visible differences (Figure 3.15).

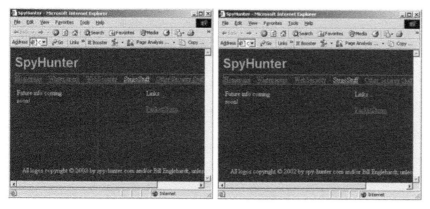

FIGURE 3.15 HTML Documents Before and After Using SNOW

In fact, viewing the file in an HTML editor, there are no obvious indications that additional data has been hidden. Only if we perform file comparisons can we find an indication that data has been hidden. Strings of tabs and spaces are evident throughout the file (Figure 3.16).

There is an online version of the tool to encrypt and decrypt HTML files with snow at http://fog.misty.com/perry/ccs/snow/snow/snow.html (Figure 3.17).

STEGANALYSIS

Digital steganalysis is the process of detecting the evidence of hidden data created by a steganographic technique or program, and when possible extract that hidden payload. If the hidden payload is also encrypted, cryptanalysis

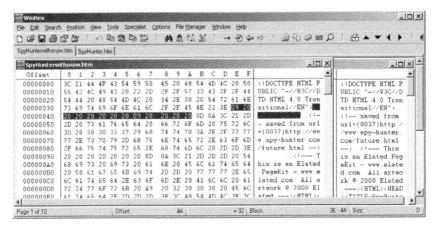

FIGURE 3.16 Using WinHex to Compare HTML Files Modified by Snow Before and After

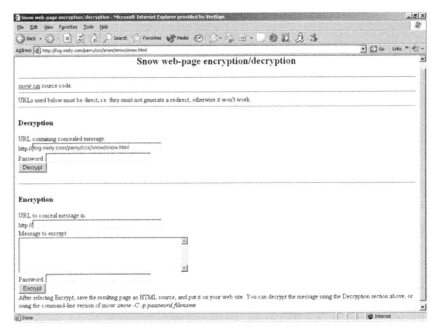

FIGURE 3.17 Online Version of Snow Tool

is required to decipher the payload. This is an important delineation and is commonly confused. Typically, one must first perform Steganalysis before performing Cryptanalysis when working with steganography (see Figure 3.18). Ideally investigators want to reveal the hidden payload, but one must note that this may require a two-step process each requiring very different techniques. One cannot typically decipher the payload without first knowing if a hidden payload exists.

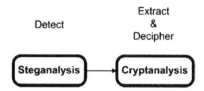

FIGURE 3.18 Steganography Analysis Process

The methods of steganalysis depend on the hiding technique. For example, the hidden data may be dispersed throughout the carrier file, but in addition to hiding the data, the steganography program may also leave behind additional trace data. The programmer may do this intentionally or unintentionally. Usually this is done so that when the same steganography program is used by the recipient to extract the hidden data, the program itself can determine first if hidden data even exists. This flaw is a definite advantage to the investigator. For example, the steganography program Hiderman appends three ASCII characters "CDN" to the end of carrier file.

This trace data is commonly referred to as a signature. Exploits and worms typically have a string of characters synonymous with their respective exploit technique. These strings are commonly used to create Instruction Detection System signatures. When the malicious code or virus passes over the wire an IDS can detect and alert the administrator. The same can be said for steganography signatures. Steganalysis scanners maintain a database of these strings and map them to known steganography programs. This provides a quick and efficient way of scanning all of the files on a suspect machine for hidden content within a file.

Scanners also exist for scanning a machine for evidence of an installed steganography program that is installed or once was installed. This could be the program executable itself, installation files, or registry entries. It is important to note that this is another form of detection, but arguably not a form of steganalysis (see Figure 3.19). Steganalysis is a process of identifying hidden content, not the process of identifying steganography programs that may be installed on a machine.

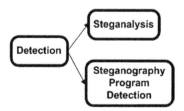

FIGURE 3.19 Forms of Steganography Detection

With over 200 documented steganography programs in the wild, it can be very difficult to reach our goal of extraction. The reason for this is that each steganography program uses its own technique for hiding, encrypting, and password protecting its content. Although there are a handful of baseline methods used to hide content, the method by which this is implemented can vary greatly across all of the available programs. Many of the same baseline methods used for hiding the content can be reversed to identify the hidden content and perform the steganalysis.

Anomalous Analysis

Anomalous analysis involves techniques used to identify differences between two similar files. It also involves analysis techniques that identify other oddities when no other file is available to compare it to.

File Properties

File property differences can easily be identified if one has both the modified file as well as the original virgin carrier file. Visually, it's impossible to detect the differences between the two pictures in Figure 3.20, but through some simple checksums and directory listings we can quickly determine differences.

Through a simple directly listing, we determine that there are discrete differences between the two files:

```
D:\dir
04/04/2012 05:25p 240,759 helmetprototype.jpg
04/04/2012 05:26p 235,750 helmetprototype.jpg
```

We note that the file sizes and creation times are different.

A simple checksum also allows us to determine that the content of the files are also different:

FIGURE 3.20 Original File and File with Hidden Data

```
C:\GNUTools>cksum a:\before\helmetprototype.jpg 3241690497 240759 a:\
   before\helmetprototype.jpg
C:\GNUTools>cksum a:\after\helmetprototype.jpg 3749290633 235750 a:\
   after\helmetprototype.jpg
```

It's important to note that there are some steganography programs which allow content to be hidden in a file, but keep the file size and creation time the same. Running a checksum on the two files, will quickly allow you determine a difference between the two files.

Steganalysis Tools

There are a variety of freeware and commercial tools that allow an investigator to perform steganalysis. Many of the freeware tools only detect a very limited set of steganography programs. The commercial tools are far more comprehensive and detect a plethora of steganography programs.

But aside from the comprehensiveness of the tool, they all have a common theme, which is to detect something about the file that may indicate that hidden content is contained within. These suspect files are then parked for a deep-dive analysis. This second phase can be part automated and part manual. The most advanced tools will also allow for manual human-in-the-loop analysis to represent the data visually to assist in detecting anomalies.

Steganography programs vary in the techniques they use for hiding data. In addition, these techniques can change with different versions of the Steganography program. This complicates the steganalysis process. To add to the complexity, some programs even use different encryption techniques when hiding the data. They can also support various file types. All of these variants must be distinguishable in the analysis so that the investigator can accurately identify the correct program and its version. By knowing both the program and its version, the investigator can proceed to reverse engineering the hiding technique to ultimately reveal the hidden message.

This chapter also covers the strengths and weaknesses of each of the tools mentioned. It is common when performing steganalysis that the investigator typically uses multiple tools. The reason is that false positives and false negatives are a common occurrence. Therefore, leveraging multiple toolsets allows the investigator to perform more accurate analysis. A collaboration of the following programs can be assembled into a comprehensive steganalysis toolkit.

Freeware Tools

Most of the freeware and open source steganalysis tools are not updated nearly as frequently as the commercial tools on the market. In addition, they are typically more point solutions effective at detecting a limited number of steganography programs and carrier files with hidden payloads. But each has their place in the investigator's toolkit. Let's look at a few.

StegSpy

URL: http://www.spy-hunter.com[10]

Description

StegSpy is a signature analysis program designed to detect the evidence of hidden content. Back in 2002, I spent a significant amount of time performing signature analysis of files with hidden content. I started by downloading and installing steganography programs and analyzing their behavior. I noticed a common trend among many steganography programs. Many programs would hide not only the message, but would embed some form of a fingerprint or string unique to the steganography program. One such example was Hiderman which (as mentioned earlier) appends three ASCII characters "CDN" to the end of the carrier file. Using this signature technique I began to build a library of the signatures, and eventually wrote a program to automate the signature analysis.

Installation

StegSpy is available as freeware from my research website: http://www.spy-hunter.com. It is written in Visual Basic and is supported on most Windows platforms (Windows 9x/ME/2000/XP). Installation is simple, it is intended to be a self-contained executable, therefore copy the executable to your machine and run the executable, thus kicking off the program as show in Figure 3.20.

Using StegSpy

When StegSpy runs it will analyze the suspect file by comparing it to a list of predefined signatures to identify hidden content. If hidden content is detected it will report what steganography program used to hide the content, and will also report where the hidden content begins within the file. This file marker is consistent with Hex editors such as WinHex. Figure 3.21 demonstrates the output of analyzing a suspect file with hidden content from the Masker steganography program.

Next, we can then open the suspect file in a hex editor to further analyze the content. The file markers reported by StegSpy are consistent with the file markers in a hex editor, making it simple to identify the location of the hidden content and focus the efforts on extracting the hidden content. Armed with this knowledge, we analyze the suspect file in a hex editor to review the content.

---

[10] Raggo, Michael—http://www.spyhunter.org.

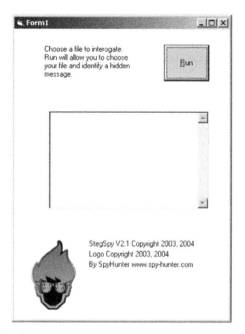

FIGURE 3.21 StegSpy Program

In this example, StegSpy identified hidden content beginning at marker position 240208. If we analyze the file in a hex editor, for example WinHex, we will see three columns (Figure 3.22). The left column is a file marker position or offset. Each character in the file represents one marker position and increments as you scroll from the beginning of the file to the end. The middle of the screen shows the file data in hexadecimal format. And the right-hand side of the screen shows the file data in text or ASCII format, same as if you viewed the file contents in Microsoft Notepad.

StegSpy detected content hidden by the Masker steganography program. In addition, it provided the marker position 240208 as the location of the beginning of the hidden content (this also indicated in Figure 3.22). This is helpful to the investigator when attempting to extract and reveal the hidden content. Identifying the location of the hidden content is only one step of the process. If the content is also encrypted, the investigator must still discover the password used to hide the content, or reverse engineer the encrypted data. For now we've succeeded in our Steganalysis—we have identified the existence of hidden content. In fact, we've also determined what program was used to hide it, and the location of the hidden content. This is particularly useful because if we know the program used to hide the data as we can use known techniques for extracting the data.

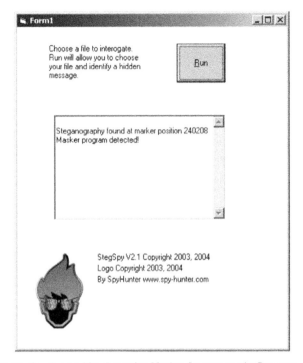

FIGURE 3.22 StegSpy Output After Detecting Masker Steganography Program

Stegdetect

URL: http://www.outguess.org/download.php[11]

Description: Stegdetect was developed by Neils Provos, highly regarded as one of the leaders in Steganalysis research having written one of the first open source steganalysis tools. He has performed extensive steganalysis research following the 9/11 attacks and has published his research in numerous articles as well as on his website. Interestingly enough, Michigan State Law has outlawed his steganography research, therefore Neils has been the center of much controversy. As a result, his research site has moved to the Netherlands. His research site can be accessed at http://niels.xtdnet.nl/stego/.

Neils Provos' steganography research is based on statistical analysis and his Stegdetect program is primarily designed to analyze JPEG files. Therefore, Stegdetect can detect content hidden by the following steganography programs: JSteg, JPHide, OutGuess, Invisible Secrets, F5, appendX, and Camouflage.

JPEG and MPEG formats use the discrete cosine transform (DCT) function to compress an image. This image compression focuses on reducing the number of

---

[11] Provos. N. Stegdetect—http://www.outguess.org/download.php.

bits needed to represent an image, by identifying duplication between adjacent pixels for every 8×8 pixel block (or in the case of MPEGs, duplication in adjacent frames in a sequence of images) and reducing this redundancy by making a mathematical approximation. Therefore, DCT can be thought of as an approximation calculation for performing compression. This image compression technique is known as a lossy compression technique since some data is lost, but is not typically intrusive to the visual representation of the picture (or video).

The tool is designed to evaluate the frequencies of the DCT coefficients of JPEG files. Stegdetect compares what it expects to be the normal frequencies for a JPEG versus what is observed in the suspect JPEG file. This of course requires some modeling and prior knowledge. Therefore, much of Neils analysis is built into his statistical algorithm. This type of analysis is also referred to as chi-square analysis. A large deviation in the comparison signifies an anomaly. This anomaly represents an above-average probability and perhaps the existence of steganography.

Installation: The Stegdetect Windows binary or source code can be downloaded from the outguess.org website. The zip file or tar includes both the command line and GUI versions of the program. In addition, Stegdetect is also found in BackTrack (https://www.backtrack-linux.com/forensics-auditor/).

Using Stegdetect

The stegdetect utility analyzes image files for steganographic content. It runs statistical tests to determine if steganographic content is present. In addition, it attempts to identify what steganography program has been used to embed the hidden information.

The significant options are as follows:

```
q - only reports images that are likely to have steganographic content.
n - enables checking of JPEG header information to surpress false
    positives. If enabled, all JPEG images that contain comment fields
    will be treated as negatives. OutGuess checking will be disabled if
    the JFIF marker does not match version 1.1.
s - changes the sensitivity of the detection algorithms. Their results
    are multiplied by the specified number. The higher the number the
    more sensitive the test will become. The default is 1.
d - num Prints debug information.
t - sets the tests that are being run on the image (default is "jopi).
    The following characters are understood:
j - tests if information has been embedded with jsteg.
o - tests if information has been embedded with outguess.
p - tests if information has been embedded with jphide.
i - tests if information has been hidden with invisible secrets.
```

If there is a positive result, the tools indicate the level of confidence with stars next to the result, ranging from one to three stars, with three starts representing a high level of confidence that there is hidden content. Ongoing analysis has shown that stegdetect is more successful with high-quality digital images, such as images from a digital camera.

The following example demonstrates using Stegdetect to scan all of the JPEG files in the current directory to determine if hidden content exists, and if so, what programs were used to embed the hidden data. In this example, the sensitivity has been increased from 1 to 10.

```
D:\>stegdetect -tjopi -s10.0 *.jpg
    bobhelmetcollwithhidden.jpg: jphide(**)
    Corrupt JPEG data: 30 extraneous bytes before marker 0xdb
    bobhelmetprototype.jpg: error: Quantization table 0x00 was not
        defined
    Corrupt JPEG data: 30 extraneous bytes before marker 0xdb
    bobhelmetprototype_withdifferentfileanddifferentpassword.jpg: error:
        Quantization table 0x00 was not defined
    bobhelmetprototypewithanotherhidden.jpg: jphide(**)
    Corrupt JPEG data: 26 extraneous bytes before marker 0xd9
    bobhelmetprototypewithhidden.jpg: jphide(**)
    familyonthecouchnormalpost.jpg: jphide(***)
    securitdaemonlogowithhiddenfile.jpg: skipped (false positive likely)
    securitydaemonlogo.jpg: invisible[4](***) skipped (false positive
        likely)
```

The output lists the analysis for each JPEG file in the directory. The stegdetect utility indicates the accuracy of the detection with a number of stars next to the detected steganography program. In the previous example, stegdetect detected jphide invisible in some of the images. It also indicated the probability for some files with two asterix and others with three.

The Stegdetect tarball or zip also includes a GUI version of the program called XSteg. All of the options are the same, so the only useful reason for using the GUI version is for the command line impaired. The next example (Figure 3.23) demonstrates a scan against the same directory of JPEG files, using all of the default switch options.

Since the defaults were left unchanged, the sensitivity was left at a value of 1. Be sure to crank the sensitivity, otherwise there will be a high occurrence of negatives as demonstrated in Figure 3.23. Changing the sensitivity from 1.00 to 10.00 produces far more accurate results as demonstrated in the next example in Figure 3.24.

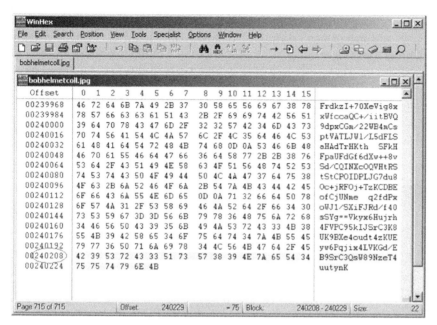

FIGURE 3.23 Suspect File Analyzed Within WinHex

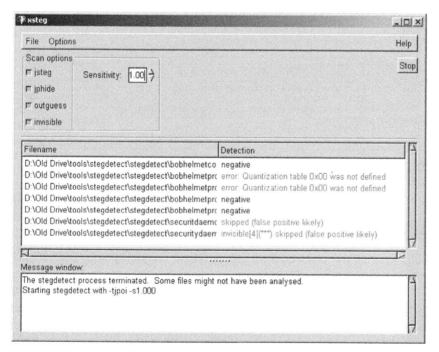

FIGURE 3.24 Xsteg Run With a Sensitivity Value of 1.

In all three previous examples, the directory chosen included numerous JPEG files, all of which contained embedded hidden content using various steganography programs. Stegdetect generated a reasonable number of false negatives and false positives. Due to the complex compression techniques employed by the JPEG format, JPEGS are particularly difficult to analyze. In addition, some JPEG steganography programs do not embed a fingerprint or signature associated with the steganography program. Therefore, in these situations Stegdetect is a unique and effective tool for analyzing JPEG files of unknown origin (see Figure 3.25).

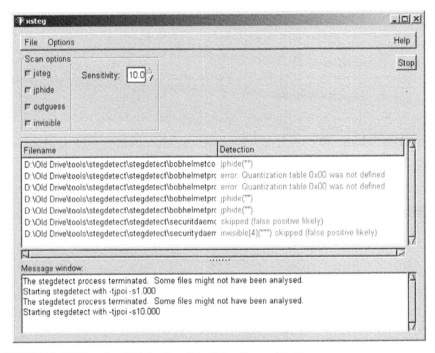

FIGURE 3.25 Xsteg Run With the Sensitivity Value Changed to 10.

SUMMARY

In this chapter, we reviewed the history of digital steganography from the mid 1990s to current day. Common steganography techniques and programs were reviewed outlining a variety of steganography methods. These methods involved hiding data in images, HTML files, and executables. As we continue our journey into data hiding we will look at many of the new ways in which data is being hidden in operating systems, multimedia, and on mobile devices.

References

JPEGX. <http://www.nerdlogic.org>.

JPEG—<http://www.findarticles.com/p/articles/mi_zdpcm/is_200409/ai_n7184572/pg_2>.

Latham. A. JPHideandSeek. <http://linux01.gwdg.de/~alatham/stego.html>.

Provos. N. Stegdetect. <http://www.outguess.org/download.php>.

Rakan, E-K. Hydan. <http://www.crazyboy.com/hydan>.

Raggo. M. StegSpy. <www.spyhunter.org>.

Revealed: Operation Shady RAT McAfee—www.mcafee.com/us/resources/white.../wp-operation-shady-rat.pdf.

Snow man page—http://www.darkside.com.au/snow/manual.html.

Snow. <www.darkside.com.au/snow/>.

The Truth Behind the Shady RAT—Symantec—http://www.symantec.com/connect/blogs/truth-behind-shady-rat.

wbStego4open. <http://wbstego.wbailer.com>.

This page is intentionally left blank

Multimedia Data Hiding

CONTENTS

MULTIMEDIA OVERVIEW

Digital music, podcasts, live and recorded webinars, video calls, and streaming video have changed the way in which we communicate, and have become ubiquitous in virtually every organization. We employ these methods to convey ideas, train our employees, engage our customers, and of course entertain. The question is, does digital multimedia pose a threat? Could these channels be used to communicate information covertly, exfiltrate intellectual property, share insider information, be used to convey command and control information, or provide the needed enabling technology for advanced persistent threats? Additionally, since the size of multimedia files are typically much larger than a single digital photo, does this mean that larger payloads of hidden information could be exchanged or leaked by exploiting weaknesses inherent in multimedia carriers? Or, on the contrary, is the human auditory system (HAS) sensitive to even small changes in multimedia information such that we could detect anomalies caused by embedding hidden information in such streams?

In this chapter, we will then cover some of the earliest and simplest forms of data hiding in digital multimedia and then move to some of the latest innovations in order to provide insight into these questions.

Data Hiding http://dx.doi.org/10.1016/B978-1-59-749743-5.00004-3

DATA HIDING IN DIGITAL AUDIO

A significant amount of research has been conducted that targets digital images as the carrier of hidden information. The HAS can make embedding more difficult due to the acute sensitivity of our hearing. According to Bender, Gruhl, and Morimoto (1996), "While the HAS has a large dynamic range, it has a fairly small differential range. As a result, loud sounds tend to mask out quiet sounds. Additionally, the HAS is unable to perceive absolute phase, only relative phase." These limitations provide the basis for the data hiding methods employed to fool our hearing. There are a couple of additional advantages as well:

1. The carrier files tend to be much larger, providing the potential to hide enormous payloads (for example, we have successfully hidden the entire works of Shakespeare in a single 8 min song).
2. The proliferation and common everyday use of mp3 files and the advent of the iPod and other music players have created an enormous haystack of digital audio files that are exchanged all over the world. I once compared finding files containing hidden information to finding a needle in a haystack. A colleague pointed out that finding a needle in the haystack would be easy. A better analogy would be trying to find a piece of straw in a haystack.

Some of the early attempts at multimedia audio data hiding focused solely on making the embedding imperceptible rather than undetectable. These methods are quite good at fooling our senses when the altered files are played. However, when we attack these simpler forms of imperceptible data hiding with statistical methods, our ability to detect them is quite effective. The big question, however, is anyone looking?

Simple Audio File Embedding (Imperceptible Approach)

One of the earliest methods of multimedia data hiding targeted raw audio files such as .wav. The most common method of digitizing audio is based on the early work of Dr. Harry Nyquist. While working at Bell Labs in the early 1920s, Nyquist determined it was not necessary to capture the complete analog waveform. Rather, samples of the analog signal could be taken and stored (see Figure 4.1). Then utilizing these samples allows for the regeneration of the original audio signal or wave.

Nyquist also determined that in order to create a quality reproduction of the original analog signal the sampling rate needed to be twice the bandwidth of the original analog wave. The fundamentals of these discoveries became the foundation of the pulse code modulation standard (PCM) to convert analog sound to digital data. This meant that a typical 4 KHz voice signal would

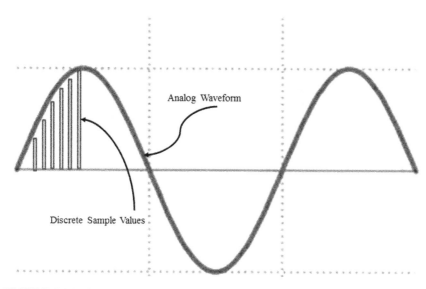

Analog Waveform

Discrete Sample Values

FIGURE 4.1 Analog Wave with Discrete Samples

be sampled 8000 times a second. To reproduce a high quality audio music recording that would fill the full Human Audio Range (22.5 Khz) the signal would need to be sampled 44,100 times per second. Since music is typically recorded in stereo (each of the two channels of audio are sampled at 44,100 samples per second. This means for every one second of stereo music 88,200 digital samples are recorded. Once recorded the original analog signal can be reproduced (approximately) through digital to analog conversion. However, these sample values can also be targeted for data hiding activities, providing a rich set of possibilities. Making this even more attractive, each of the 88,200 samples per second are typically recorded as a 16 bit signed integer values, −32,768–+32,767. Thus modification of the Least Significant Bit (LSB) will make only slight changes to the analog rendering, making this an ideal candidate for data hiding.

The resulting wave file (.wav) has a very specific and defined format that it is quite flexible and is still relied upon today for digital recording and transmission. Most .wav files we utilize have a slightly simplified format that only require a format segment and a data segment. In Figure 4.2, we have annotated an actual audio recording. We defined the length of each field, provided a short description of the field, and then noted the endian of each value, so we can determine how to interpret them.

> *Important header values include:*
> *Audio Type:* WAVE.
> *Modulation method:* In this example PCM is specified.

Value				Description	Endian
R	I	F	F	File ID	Big
28	5c	67	00	Segment Size	Little
W	A	V	E	Audio Type	Big
f	m	t		Start Format Segment	Big
10	00	00	00	Modulation Method = PCM	Little
01	00			Quantization = Linear	Little

Value				Description	Endian
02	00			Channels = 2 or Stereo	Little
44	ac	00	00	44,100 Samples / Sec	Little
10	b1	02	00	Byte Rate	Little
04	00			Block Align = 4 Bytes	Little
10	00			Bits Per Sample = 16	Little
d	a	t	a	Start Data Segment	Big
04	5c	67	00	Size of Data Segment	Little

```
Offset      0  1  2  3  4  5  6  7   8  9  A  B  C  D  E  F
00000000   52 49 46 46 28 5C 67 00  57 41 56 45 66 6D 74 20   RIFF(\g WAVEfmt
00000010   10 00 00 00 01 00 02 00  44 AC 00 00 10 B1 02 00           D⁻   ±
00000020   04 00 10 00 64 61 74 61  04 5C 67 00 00 00 00 00        data \g
```

FIGURE 4.2 Example Wave File Header

Number of Channels: 2. This is what we typically see for the majority of music files.

The Sampling Rate: 44,100 for each channel (based on Nyquist's theorem).

The Number of bytes for each sample and the number of bits utilized.

Next the start of the continuous data is marked, and the length of the data is specified. The length is defined as a 4 byte hexadecimal value 04-5C-67-00. To derive the number of samples per channel, we first convert 04-5C-67-00 hex value from little endian to big endian by swapping both bytes and words, obtaining the length equal to 00-67-5C-04 Hex or 6,737,476 Decimal. Since there are two channels defined in this example we divide this value by two resulting in 3,386,882 bytes for each channel. Each recorded sample requires 16 bits or 2 bytes yielding 1,693,441 samples per channel. Note the audio clip chosen for this example is 38s in length. We could have also arrived at this sample count by multiplying 38s × 44,100 samples per second (see Figure 4.3).

Next, we examine the individual data values. We break the first few samples into Left and Right channels. We then convert the little endian values to big

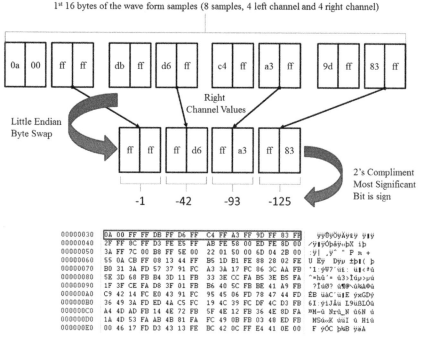

FIGURE 4.3 Example Wave Sample Data

endian, and take the 2s complement of each 16 bit value, preserving the most significant bit as the sign. If the most significant bit is 1, then the value is considered negative. We further decoded the sample and derive the first four Right channel values as -1, -42, -93, and -125. If we render the wave form in StegoAnalyst we can see the waveform generated by the entire 38 s music clip (see Figure 4.4).

By electing to view just a portion of the waveform, (in this case values 1 to 4) (see Figure 4.5) we can see that the individual samples match the values we extracted and converted manually from the raw data.

Data hiding in a .wav file

Now that we have a firm grasp on how .wav files are constructed, we understand the basic principles of Nyquist theorem and how this theorem was the driving force behind pulse code modulation, and we also understand that sample values are stored as alternating signed 16 bit integers; we are now ready to hide information in the .wav file. As you may have already guessed, we can modify the Least Significant Bit (LSB) of the 16 bit integer values to encode a

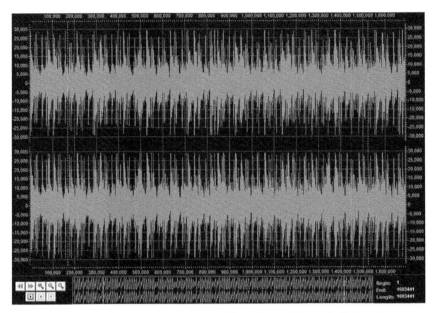

FIGURE 4.4 Wave Audio File with Left (Top) and Right (Bottom) Channels All Samples

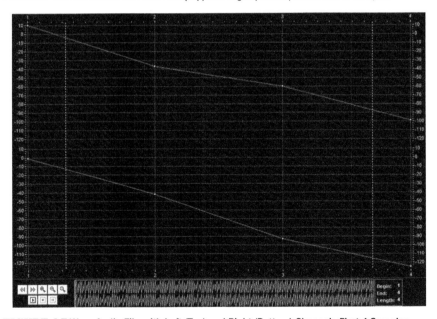

FIGURE 4.5 Wave Audio File with Left (Top) and Right (Bottom) Channels First 4 Samples

hidden message. In Figure 4.5, we have extracted the first eight right channel samples for the .wav used in our illustration. We then converted the sample values from little endian to big endian and substituted the LSB value for each bit of the binary representation of the ASCII capital 'A'. This illustration results in two important observations:

1. The substitution of one 8 bit ASCII character requires the use of eight sample values from the Wave data.
2. Note that in this example only five of the eight values actually changed, as three of the LSB values were already in the right state. Therefore the substitution causes no perceptible change to the associated LSB. For typical LSB substitutions when random data is inserted (most data hiding/steganography programs first compress then encrypt the data prior to embedding, thus creating pseudorandomness) the substitution rate will be approximately 50%. If you need to hide 8000 bytes the hiding will likely only modify $\sim$ 32,000 samples not 64,000 (see Figure 4.6).

Now let's examine the operation of an audio steganography application in action. We are going to use S-TOOLS version 4.0. The first step is to select a .wav file to use as the carrier file. We will choose the same file we have been examining manually *Sample Wave.wav*. In Figure 4.7 below, we have dragged the *Sample Wav.wav* file into the S-TOOLS window, and S-TOOLS displays a graphical representation of the waveform. Notice in the bottom right, S-TOOLS has calculated the maximum payload that this specific .wav file can hold, 423,352 bytes. This value is the available space after compression. This is the total number of bytes that can be hidden. Recall previously we calculated the

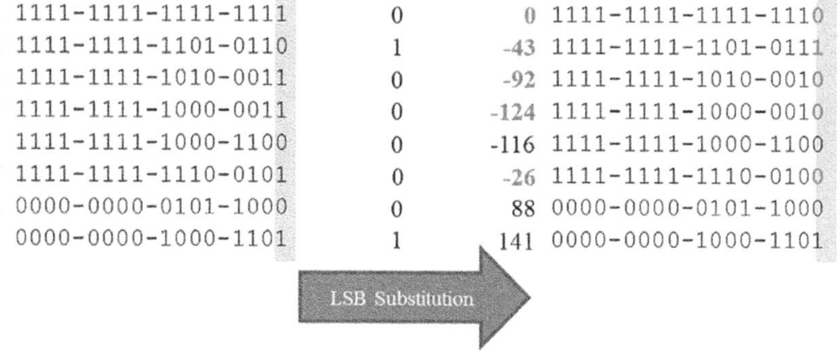

FIGURE 4.6 Least Significant Bit Substitution of Wave Samples

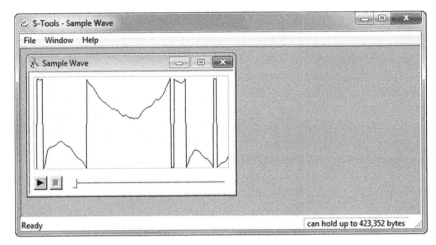

FIGURE 4.7 STOOLS v 4.0 with Sample Wave Ready for Data Hiding

total sample values (for both channels) as 3,386,882. Thus, if we divide this by 8 (the number of samples needed to encode each 8 bit byte), we get 423,360. This would leave eight 16 bit values unmodified or unavailable for embedding. The S-TOOLS program reserves these unmodified values for program usage.

As shown in Figure 4.8, prior to the data hiding operation S-TOOLS provides the ability to perform encryption using a password-based key. You may select from several encryption algorithms for this example. We choose Triple DES.

Once the data hiding has been accomplished, S-TOOLS provides a display of the two waveforms (see Figure 4.9 below) side by side to permit a cursory

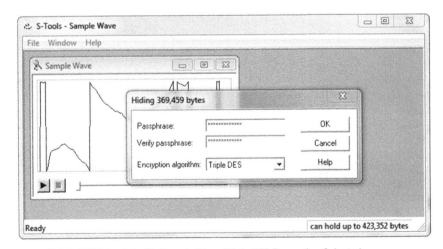

FIGURE 4.8 STOOLS v 4.0 with Sample Wave, Triple DES Encryption Selected

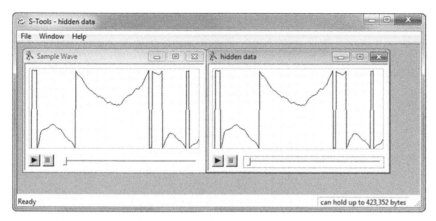

FIGURE 4.9 STOOLS v 4.0 after Data Hiding Wave Form Comparison

check that the embedding did not make major waveform adjustments during the hiding process. You may also listen to each of the samples to compare the audio quality of each recording and attempt to discern any differences.

Now let's examine the before and after image with StegAnalyst and take a close look at the modifications that were made. In Figure 4.10, we are taking a close look at the first eight samples in order to examine the modifications that were made to the original. We have highlighted the values recorded for the third sample. In the original, the sample value was −125 and the value has changed to −126 demonstrating the LSB substitution.

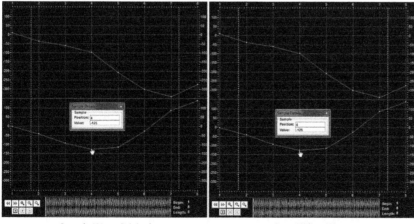

Sample Wave Original   Data Hiding Wave

FIGURE 4.10 Analysis of the Original vs. Data Hiding Waveform

```
Offset      0  1  2  3  4  5  6  7   8  9 10 11 12 13 14 15
00000000   52 49 46 46 28 5C 67 00  57 41 56 45 66 6D 74 20   RIFF(\g WAVEfmt
00000016   10 00 00 00 01 00 02 00  44 AC 00 00 10 B1 02 00           D¬   ±
00000032   04 00 10 00 64 61 74 61  04 5C 67 00 00 00 00 00     data \g
00000048   0A 00 FF FF DB FF D6 FF  C4 FF A3 FF 9D FF 83 FF     ÿÿÛÿÖÿ Äÿ£ÿ  ÿ ÿ
00000064   2F FF 8C FF D3 FE E5 FF  AB FE 58 00 ED FE 8D 00   /ÿ ÿ Óþåÿ«þX íþ
```

Sample Wave Original Header and Start of Sample Data Values

```
Offset      0  1  2  3  4  5  6  7   8  9  A  B  C  D  E  F
00000000   52 49 46 46 28 5C 67 00  57 41 56 45 66 6D 74 20   RIFF(\g WAVEfmt
00000010   10 00 00 00 01 00 02 00  44 AC 00 00 10 B1 02 00           D¬   ±
00000020   04 00 10 00 64 61 74 61  04 5C 67 00 00 00 00 00     data \g
00000030   0A 00 FE FF DA FF D6 FF  C4 FF A3 FF 9D FF 82 FF   bÿÛÿÖÿÄÿ£ÿ  ÿ ÿ
00000040   2E FF 8D FF D3 FE E5 FF  AB FE 58 00 ED FE 8D 00   . ÿ ÿÓþåÿ«þX íþ
```

Sample Wave Data Hiding Example Header and Start of Sample Data Values

FIGURE 4.11 Analysis of the Original vs. Data Hiding Hex Data

Finally, in Figure 4.11 below we have included the Hex dump of the header and the first 16 sample values of both the left and right channel. By close examination you can identify each LSB substitution that was made by S-TOOLS.

StegAnalysis of LSB Wave Data Hiding

LSB Data Hiding in wave files provides excellent imperceptible data hiding. In other words, by listening to the original wave and then the stego'd wave even a highly trained ear could not discern the difference. If one had the original recording and could compare the two files it would be easy to identify the changes. Based on the changes between the two waves, one could deduce that LSB data hiding had been applied. However, in most cases we only have the modified or stego'd wave file to examine. In this case, our approach must be to determine that LSB modification has been made without the assistance of the original recording. In other words, what would prevent LSB embedding from being undetectable vs. imperceptible. The *basic fundamental* is the LSB values of the original samples contained *information* not random noise. For example, if we were to extract out the LSB values of each sample the values would contain some remnant of the music. Therefore, the key to detecting LSB Wave file embedding is to determine if the LSB's values in the Wave file under examination contain information or simply random noise. A common method for making this determination is to estimate the compressibility of the resulting bit stream. In the case of wave audio files you would extract the LSB of each channel and then perform a statistical analysis test for example (Mauer, 1990). The Maurer test was originally developed to evaluate the quality of random number generators used in cryptographic applications and provides the "quality of the randomness." We can use this to then determine how random the data contain in the LSB of audio wave file is.

One way to defeat LSB audio data hiding would be to employ an active Warden. The Warden would then zero the LSB values of a specific number of samples. This would not cause perceptible changes in the audio playback, but would effectively render the channel useless.

Advanced Audio File Embedding

Moving ahead a decade in time, the advancements in audio embedding have been slow to develop. Even today only a handful of data hiding and steganography programs exist that support common compressed audio files such as MP3 or AAC. The most notable is MP3Stego which utilizes a special quantization method and then hides the data within the parity blocks of an MP3 File. The MP3 Encoder takes a .wav file as input along with a payload file to hide and generates a resulting .mp3 file. Significant limitations exist in the size of the payload file. For example, a sample full spectrum audio wave file of just under 6 megabytes can hide a payload of less than 6 Kilobytes, or approximately 0.1% (see Figure 4.12).

```
MP3StegoEncoder 1.1.15
See README file for copyright info
USAGE   :   encode [options] <infile> <outfile>
OPTIONS :  -h                this help message
           -b <bitrate>   set the bitrate, default 128kbit
           -c                set copyright flag, default off
           -o                set original flag, default off
           -E <filename> name of the file to be hidden
           -P <text>       passphrase used for embedding
```

```
MP3StegoEncoder 1.1.15
See README file for copyright info
Microsoft RIFF, WAVE audio, PCM, stereo 44100Hz 16bit, Length:  0: 0:38
MPEG-I layer III, stereo  Psychoacoustic Model: AT&T
Bitrate=128 kbps  De-emphasis: none  CRC: off
Encoding "inwave.wav" to "sample.mp3"
Hiding "simpleinsert.txt"
Enter a passphrase:
Confirm your passphrase:
[Frame   1470 of   1470] (100.00%) Finished in  0: 0:16
```

FIGURE 4.12 MP3Stego Command Line MP3 Encoder

Audio Summary

The evolution of audio data hiding has been slow yet steady, moving from simple LSB embedding that provides large payload capabilities with imperceptibility to the HAS to MP3 encoding that provides little in the way of payload capacity, but can provide both imperceptibility and challenges to detection. The bigger thrust today is the application of advanced audio hiding methods that work on smartphones, providing steganography/data hiding on the go. We will discuss this in more depth in the Android Data Hiding Chapter as the evolution of data hiding methods is moving to Android SmartPhone-based technologies that employ advanced echo-based data hiding that improves upon payload size over other compressed audio embedding and also increases the difficulty in detection.

We expect to see improvements in the robustness of LSB embedding that relies on spread- spectrum methods, advanced randomization schemes, and targeted hiding approaches that will make entropy detection more difficult while maintain the payload size advantages. We also expect improvement in hiding methods that focus on AAC and MP3 files that will make slight modification to the encoded compressed data that will increase payload capacity without sacrificing robustness.

Finally, we will see additional audio methods that are deployed to which smart mobile devices. These will provide data hiding or steganography on the go applications for criminals and others with new weapons for covert communications.

DATA HIDING IN DIGITAL VIDEO

Digital video-based data hiding or steganography has significant potential as a primary covert communication channel. This is mainly due to the larger size, the sheer number of videos that are streamed today and the ubiquitous nature of virtual video exchange over the Internet or via the cloud. This medium is and will continue to be a target of those wishing to cloak and conceal their communications. Digital video has two basic forms, compressed and uncompressed. We will first examine MSUStego with uncompressed frames from an AVI video. We will then examine compressed video. The most popular form of compressed video is the Motion Compensated Compressed Video Format or MPEGx. MPEG achieves high compression rates by eliminating statistical redundancies (both temporal and spatial). The resulting video bit stream is made up of variable length codes that represent the video through various segmentation methods.

MSU Stego

Overview of MSU StegoVideo:

MSU StegoVideo is a free *non-open* source steganography program available from Moscow State University in Russia. The key features of this application include:

1. The ability to hide information in full motion video.
2. The information hidden by MSU Stego is redundantly embedded throughout frames of movie. This makes the resulting Audio Video Interleave

FIGURE 4.13 MSU Stego Usage Hiding Example

FIGURE 4.14 MSU Stego Usage Hiding Example

(AVI) file resilient to data loss (for example, if packets were lost during a streaming transmission) [Microsoft].

3. MSU Stego provides imperceptible changes to the video when viewing in normal or high definition modes.

4. The embedding method attempts to keep the changes to each video frame small in order to attempt stealthy or undetectable data hiding.

In Figure 4.13, we demonstrate the simple usage of the MSU data hiding process:

1. First, we define whether we intend to hide or extract data.

2. Next, we specific the three files that MSU Stego requires:

    a. The input file or original video (this must be in an AVI container).

    b. The output file where you would like the resulting video to be stored.

    c. The information you would like to hide (currently this must be a text .txt file containing only ASCII data).

    In our example, we are using a video clip that we extracted from the Disney Movie Tron. The clip that we are using is only 32 s in length. MSU Stego tells us the maximum size of the payload file is 2177 bytes and we have constructed a randomly generated text file with exactly 2177 bytes.

3. Next, we specify the noise level and data redundancy level. The data redundancy level will determine how many duplicates of the data that will be inserted to aid in recovery due to lost or corrupted frames.

4. Finally, produce the new AVI file.

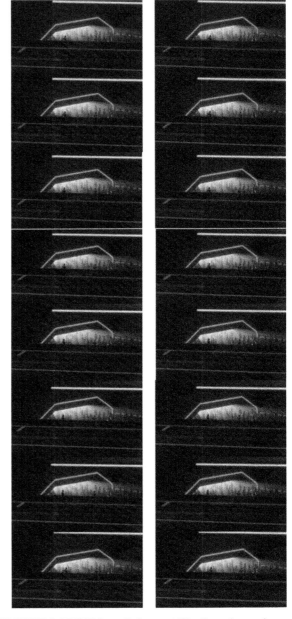

FIGURE 4.15 MSU Stego Before and After Fame Comparison

In Figure 4.14 below, we reverse the process and extract hidden information.

In order to analyze the effectiveness of the data hiding activities, we must examine each individual frame of the video (before and after). In Figure 4.15 below, we have extracted a sequence of frames

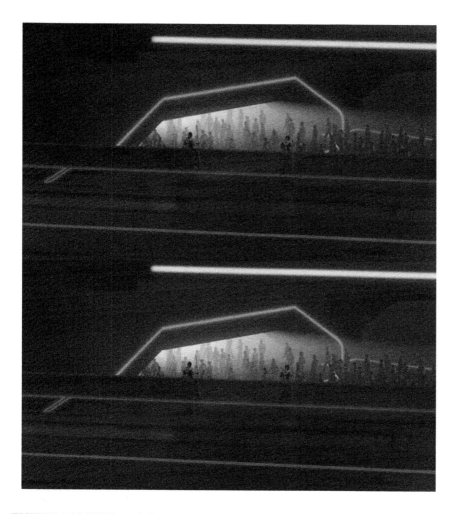

FIGURE 4.16 MSU Stego Before and After Fame Comparison with Zoom

from the video and compared them. As you can see we have extracted eight frames of the video and to the naked eye they look identical. Even in Figure 4.16 we have zoomed in on only a single frame and the before and after are indistinguishable.

In Figure 4.17, we have used StegAnalyst to render only the LSB of the resulting color data, White areas indicate a value of '1' for the LSB of that pixel, while Black represent pixels with a LSB value of '0'. MSU Stego is known to target '0' value LSB's. As shown in the StegAnalyst screen shot, we have zoomed in 2000 times in order to examine the video frame at the pixel level. The image on the right depicts the frame that contains the hidden data, while the image on the left is the original. We have illustrated the individual pixels that were modified by MSU Stego to hide the text payload.

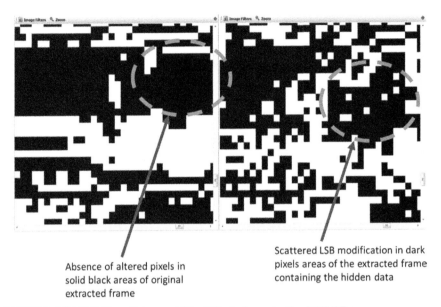

Absence of altered pixels in
solid black areas of original
extracted frame

Scattered LSB modification in dark
pixels areas of the extracted frame
containing the hidden data

FIGURE 4.17 MSU Stego Before and After LSB pixel examination 2000 X Zoom

TCStego

One of the latest weapons is a new technology that combines the power of TrueCrypt® (one of the best known and easy to use encryption programs) with a steganography twist. This latest advancement hides a TrueCrypt container inside an existing MP4 or QuickTime multimedia file.

The software application tcsteg.py is referred to as; *TrueCrypt real steganography tool* by the developer Martin J. Fiedler. The application is a straightforward python script and provided to the world under an open source license with some restrictions. The python application is simple to use and works with both QuickTime and MP4 multimedia containers.

The tcsteg.py application combines an existing MP4 or QuickTime multimedia file with a TrueCrypt file container in such a manner that the resulting file operates as both as a standard multimedia file or as a mountable TrueCrypt volume.

This operation allows one to covertly embed a TrueCrypt container inside an existing QuickTime or MP4 movie, without affecting the operational characteristics of the movie. In other words the movie still plays, the size of the movie does increase slightly based on the hidden container, but nothing that would be noticed through casual inspection. It is quite difficult to detect the presence of the embedded TrueCrypt container without specialized detection technology (if anyone is actually looking for information hidden in such a manner). Even when the hidden TrueCrypt container is detected, the ability to extract the hidden information is nearly impossible without knowledge of the key used to encrypt the hidden TrueCrypt volume.

With the rapid increase in movie files exchanged over the Internet (YouTube, etc.) a huge haystack to hide or exchange covert information exists right now today, and this is predicted to increase exponentially over the next decade. Clearly this provides a new method for pedophiles to exchange their content through innocuous sharing of benign looking digital media, and for criminals or worse to continually exchange large amounts of clandestine information.

In Figure 4.18, you see a *simplified* structure of a typical Movie File (I stress simplified as a detailed description would require a whole book). The Media Data (MDAT) and the Sample Table Chunk Offset (STOC) are the key components of the existing multimedia that are used to facilitate the hiding. The MDAT contains the actual raw audio / video data. The MDAT chunks can vary in length and are not required to be in any particular order. The STCO is a table of references that allows for the MDAT to exist in a non-ordered manner. STCO block contains pointers to the starting positions of chunks within the MDAT. This flexibility has many advantages including: quick editing,

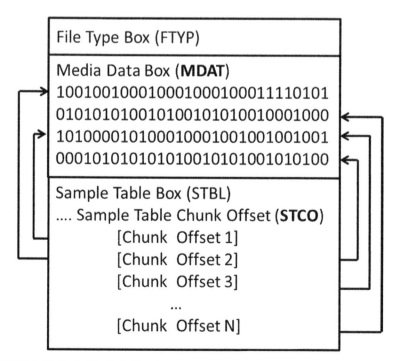

FIGURE 4.18 Movie File Basic Structure

seeking, local playback, and capabilities for video streaming. Reordering of samples can be done swiftly and easily by simply changing a pointer in the STCO. Thus, any seeking in the file requires consultation of the STCO for the correct MDAT chunk locations. When playing a movie this is what allows us to seek to specific portions of the movie, fast forward, rewind, or remember where we were when we press pause. Through the manipulation of the MDAT and STCO, tcsteg.py can embed a chunk that does not actually contain raw video or audio, but rather contains the content of the TrueCrypt hidden volume.

As you can see in Figure 4.19, the structure of the movie file is slightly altered by tcsteg.py. In order for this to work, the TrueCrypt container must contain both an outer and hidden volume. The outer volume is thrown away during

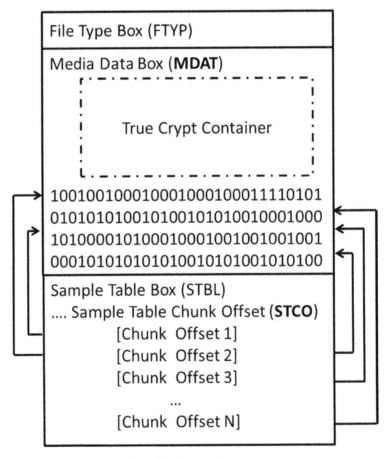

FIGURE 4.19 Movie File with Hidden TrueCrypt Container

the process of embedding to further disguise the hiding, but the inner or hidden volume remains intact. TCTSTEG also adds some spoofed data to make MDAT seem legitimate. Thus if you were to view the media file with a hex editor, you would not find anything suspicious about the MDAT. At this point the media file will play and operate as you would expect, but if you attempt to mount the media file using TrueCrypt (see Figure 4.20) and supply the correct password it operates correctly as a hidden container.

As you would suspect, discovering such hybrid media/TrueCrypt files can be accomplished programmatically, if you are looking of course. The discovery involves analyzing the 'STCO' and the 'MDAT' section of the multimedia file. By examining each Chunk Offset contained in the STCO all of the data contained in the MDAT should be accounted for. An orphaned region is an obvious anomaly because the decoder would never attempt to play or seek to that region. By identifying the gap created by the insertion of the TrueCrypt container we can also then estimate the size of the orphan region.

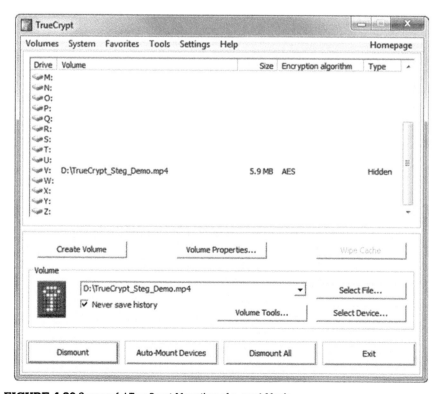

FIGURE 4.20 Successful TrueCrypt Mounting of a .mp4 Movie

The simple python script below will detect such anomalies.

```python
#!/usr/bin/env python
#
# Data Hiding Book 2012
# Code is published as Open Source, provided the Book and Authors are Reference
#
# James Bettke and Chet Hosmer
#
# JPEG EOF Payload Extractor
#
# usage jpegEOFx.py <INPUT JPEG> <OUTPUT PAYLOAD>
#

import sys
import struct
import os

# JPEG Segment markers

SOI  = 0xFFD8  # Start Of Image - Fixed size
SOF0 = 0xFFC0  # Start Of Frame (Baseline DCT)
SOF2 = 0xFFC2  # Start Of Frame (Progressive DCT)
DHT  = 0xFFC4  # Define Huffman Table(s)
DQT  = 0xFFDB  # Define Quantization Table(s)
DRI  = 0xFFDD  # Define Restart Interval
SOS  = 0xFFDA  # Start Of Scan
RST0 = 0xFFD0  # Restart (0-7) - Fixed size
APP0 = 0xFFE0  # Application-specific (0-F)
COM  = 0xFFFE  # Comment
EOI  = 0xFFD9  # End Of Image - Fixed size

RST_MASK = 0xFFD8
APP_MASK = 0xFFF0
FIELD_LENGTH = 2


# Parse JPEG segments until the end of image marker is
# encountered. Returns the Payload as a string.

def extractPayload(fp):

    fp.seek(0)

    offset = 0
    length = None
    startOfPayload = 0

    while True:

        offset = fp.tell()

        # Read segment marker
        marker = struct.unpack(">H", fp.read(2))[0]

        # Handle variable size segments with trailing length field
        if marker in [SOF0,SOF2,DHT,DQT,DRI,COM] or (marker&APP_MASK)==APP0:

            # Read length Big-endian int16
            length = struct.unpack(">H", fp.read(2))[0]

            # Seek to next segment marker
            fp.seek(length - FIELD_LENGTH, 1)

        # Handle fixed size segments
        elif marker in [SOI,EOI] or (marker&RST_MASK)==RST0:
            length = FIELD_LENGTH

        # entropy-coded data, any 0xFF byte will be followed by 0x00 unless it
is a marker
```

```
        elif marker == SOS:

            # Read file remainder into buffer
            buff = fp.read()

            # Search until EOI marker is found
            eoi_pos = buff.find("\xFF\xD9")

            if eoi_pos < 0:
                print >>sys.stderr, "ERROR: Corrupt JPEG. Cannot find End of
Image marker."
                return None
            else:
                return buff[ eoi_pos + FIELD_LENGTH: ]

        # Hanlde unknown markers
        else:
            print >>sys.stderr, "ERROR: Unknown makrer 0x" + hex(marker&0xFFFF)
            sys.exit(1)
        #endif

    #endwhile

    return None
#enddef



if __name__ == "__main__":

    if len(sys.argv) < 3:
        print "Usage: jpegEOFx.py <INPUT JPEG> <OUTPUT PAYLOAD>"
        sys.exit(2)

    jpegFile = open(sys.argv[1], "rb")

    # Check if file is JPEG
    if jpegFile.read(2) != "\xFF\xD8":
        print >>sys.stderr, "ERROR: File is not a JPEG image."
        sys.exit(1)

    payload = extractPayload(jpegFile)

    # Write payload to output file
    if payload:
        print "Found an extra",len(payload),"bytes after End of Image marker."
        outFile = open(sys.argv[2], "wb")
        outFile.write(payload)
        outFile.close()

    jpegFile.close()

    JPEG End of Marker Python Script
```

Source Code—1 Python script for identifying structural anomolies within QuickTime or MPEG Movie Files such as TCStego.

SUMMARY

Hiding information in video files such as uncompressed AVI and compressed MPEGx is not only possible today, but can provide a significantly sized container that would allow for continuous transmission of hidden data. With current and future innovations in error correction and data redundancy that will allow for the hidden data to survive under even noisy line conditions, streaming of hiding information would certainly enter a new level of threat. The Stego Analyst then has the arduous task of detection or at least jamming these covert channels to prevent against covert communications, exfiltration of intellectual property or the use of streaming channels for command and control of other malicious code that could accelerate / facilitate advanced persistent threats.

References

Bender, W., Gruhl, D., & Morimoto, N. (1996). Techniques for data hiding. *IBM Systems Journal*, *35*(3&4), 893–896. 55

Mauer, U. M. A universal statistical test for random bit generators. *Institute for Theoretical Computer Science*, ETH Ziirich, CH-8092 Ziirich, Switzerland 2 April 1990 and revised 23 June 1991.

## CHAPTER 5

Data Hiding Among Android Mobile Devices

INFORMATION IN THIS CHAPTER:

- Android Overview
- Android ImgHid and Reveal App
- Android My Secret App
- StegDroid

CONTENTS

ANDROID OVERVIEW

In this chapter, we will utilize two specific images, one as the carrier and one as the hidden payload. As illustrated in Figures 5.1 and 5.2.

For the examples in this chapter, we are using a Droid X device containing Android OS version: 2.3 and associated data hiding applications. All the selected apps have been downloaded from the Android Marketplace.

Many data hiding applications exist on the plethora of Android OS related devices and in examining the techniques and characteristics of each, we have selected just a few to include in this chapter that demonstrate unique data hiding techniques. They include:

1. ImgHid and reveal.
2. My Secret.
3. StegDroid.

ANDROID IMGHID AND REVEAL APP

The Android Image Hide (ImgHid) and Reveal App provides the capability to insert one photo inside another. This application, like most of the image-based data hiding Android apps, prefers the use of JPEG files. This differs from the

91

FIGURE 5.1 Android Carrier Image

FIGURE 5.2 Standard Payload Image

iPhone apps that prefer PNG files as data hiding targets. Since development of Java-based apps on Android is both popular and straightforward and due to the plethora of Java-based JPEG algorithms and manipulation capabilities, this has made this a popular choice.

Image Hide and Reveal Details	
Application Name	**ImgHid and Reveal**
Developer/creator	actfor-j
Carrier format	JPEG
Last release	July 2011

As with most Android and iPhone apps, the interface and operation is easy. The ImgHid navigation screen is displayed in Figure 5.3. We will be selecting the ImgHid option to get started with the data hiding operation.

For ImgHid you first must define what image or photograph you wish to hide, in other words the secret image. In Figure 5.4, you can see we selected the guns and ammo image we plan to hide.

FIGURE 5.3 ImgHid Navigation Screenshot

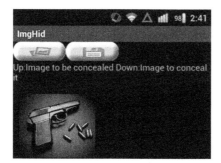

FIGURE 5.4 ImgHid Selection of Secret Image Screenshot

Using the Gallery (Figure 5.5) again, we also select the standard Snow Owl image as our cover or the carrier of the hidden payload. Now both the gun and ammo image and the Snow Owl image results are shown in Figure 5.6.

At this point, we are ready to combine the images. ImgHid performs the data hiding operation and the secret image (gun and ammo) is successfully hidden inside the Snow Owl image as seen in Figure 5.7.

At this point, we simply return to the navigation bar where you can utilize your E-mail client to distribute the resulting image that contains the hidden image, as shown in Figure 5.8.

Now we are ready to analyze the result.

FIGURE 5.5 ImgHid Gallery Screenshot

FIGURE 5.6 ImgHid Secret and Carrier

FIGURE 5.7 ImgHid Successful Completion of the Data Hiding Operation

FIGURE 5.8 ImgHid Execution of Data Hiding Screenshot

Analysis of the Resulting ImgHid Data Hiding Operation

In order to examine the method and sophistication of ImgHid, we first take a look at the resulting image and compare it to the original Snow Owl image we started with. In Figure 5.9, we can see several dramatic differences before and after. The original Snow Owl image is on the left and the image containing the hidden gun and ammo image is on the right.

Differences:

1. Image dimensions have been scaled down considerably.
2. The size of the stego'd image is also smaller.

Taking a closer look at the header of the image file in Figure 5.10, we see that all the metadata that was included in the original Snow Owl image has been removed.

FIGURE 5.9 Basic Before and After Image Details

FIGURE 5.10 Snow Owl Before and After Metadata Examination

Next, we examine the common JPEG markers to determine if any anomalies exist. We see in Figure 5.11 immediately that the original image on the left has the proper end of image marker FF D9 at the end of the file. This marker signifies the end of the data and should be last content of a properly formed JPEG. As you can see the same FF D9 marker does exist in the stego'd image on the right, however, additional data is written after the end marker signifying data appending.

Now that we have determined that the steganography method employed by ImgHid is one of the Data Appending after the JPEG End Marker we compare two ImgHid stego'd images. Both Images started with exactly the same Snow Owl image but used different payloads. In Figure 5.12, we compare the two Snow Owls with only different payloads. The image on the left used a ribbons payload and the image on the right attempted to hide the guns and ammo image. As you can see the resulting image characteristics are almost exactly the same in all cases, size, geometry, used colors, etc.

Taking a close look at the content of the two stego'd images reveals a pattern that will not only allow us to detect that data hiding exists for these two images, but also determine the source of the data hiding is ImgHid. As you can see in Figure 5.13, the two stego'd images both start with hex bytes after the FF D9:

> 55 45 73 44 42 42 51 41 43 41 67 49

And they both end with:

> 41 41 41 41 3D 3D

FIGURE 5.11 Snow Owl Before and After End of File Marker Examination

FIGURE 5.12 ImgHid Comparable Stego'd Images

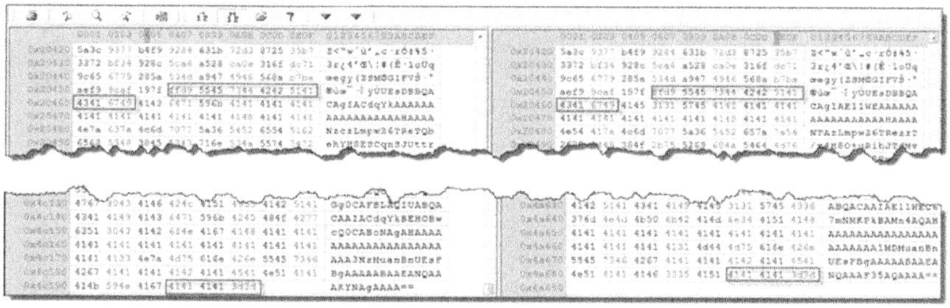

FIGURE 5.13 ImgHid Hex JPEG Marker Comparison of Two Stego'd Images

For all the images and payloads we tested the patterns were the same.

The content and data between these beginning and end markers contains a proprietary encoding of the hidden image file, in our case the guns and ammo image. What is important to note is the resulting payload, once extracted, has also been reduced significantly in resolution and dimensionally changed through the data hiding processes. Figure 5.14 depicts the original guns and ammo image alongside the extract hidden payload from the Snow Owl.

In summary, the ImgHid Android app, is simple to use and provides good basic data hiding characteristics, in other words the image looks good under

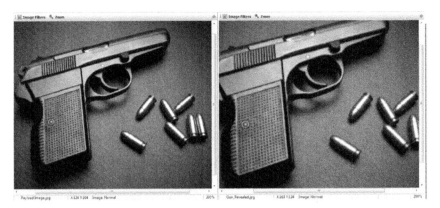

FIGURE 5.14 Before and After Extraction Guns and Ammo Payload

normal rendering. However, detailed examination reveals the common data appending method which is easy to identify and traces back to the ImgHid app.

ANDROID MY SECRET APP

Android My Secret App Details	
Application Name	**My Secret**
Developer/creator	Tipspedia Ro
Carrier format	JPEG
Last release	September 2011

As with the previous iPhone and Android Apps My Secret offers ease of use, so we will move quickly through the application operational sequence in order to get to the analysis of the data hiding method.

The navigation screen depicted in Figure 5.15, provides selections to create or read secret images.

By selecting Create Secret, we move to the screen shown below in Figure 5.16. Here we click in the black region of the app to select the carrier image that will be used for data hiding operations.

We select the Snow Owl once again as our carrier or cover image as shown in Figure 5.17.

Since My Secret provides the ability to hide a text message only inside an image carrier, we type in our standard secret emergency broadcast message. We also can if we wish, specify an optional password. This is displayed in Figure 5.18.

FIGURE 5.15 My Secret Navigation Screenshot

FIGURE 5.16 My Secret Carrier Selection Screenshot

FIGURE 5.17 My Secret Carrier Selected Screenshot

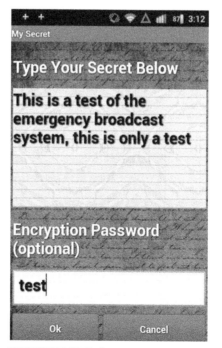

FIGURE 5.18 My Secret Message Entry Screenshot

Stego Analysis of the Resulting My Secret Images

Analyzing the My Secret hiding method involves similar steps. First, let's take a look at the images and the basic geometry. Figure 5.19 shows that both images are almost identical in size, the geometry matches perfectly. In addition, the two images displayed are identical even under close inspections and multiple renderings and magnification.

Next, we examine the metadata found in the headers of both images, again we find no modifications. Based on this we can deduce several facts:

1. It is unlikely that the image was re-encoded, therefore modifications to the quantized DCT is unlikely.
2. Prepending of data in the header of the JPEG is also unlikely as the meta data and header areas of the image match perfectly.

Examining the other JPEG markers, such as end of file, does reveal modification. As you can see in Figure 5.20, the original carrier image has the proper FF D9 end marker at the end of the file. However, the stego'd image does not, and most importantly contains a small amount of information consistent with the size of the emergency broadcast message that was hidden.

FIGURE 5.19 My Secret Stego Analyst Image Display and Geometry Comparison

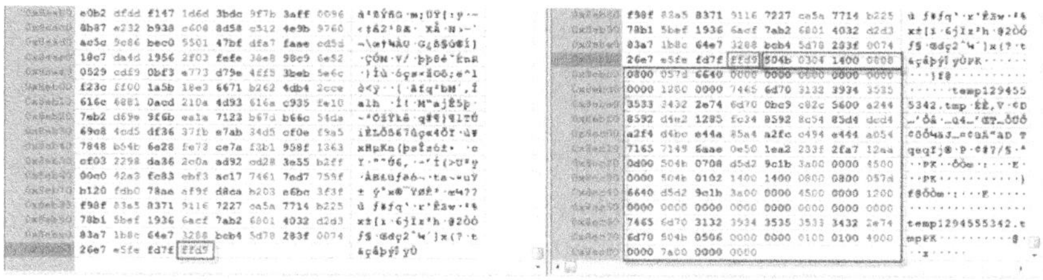

FIGURE 5.20 Before and After Comparison of the JPEG End of File Marker

Summary

The My Secret Android App accomplish hiding of information in an efficient manner and causes zero visual changes to the rendered image under any amount of scrutiny. However, once again by examining the common JPEG markers, we find data appending operations, this time of the encoded text which results in a much smaller payload. As with the ImgHid application, signatures can be derived from the data hiding operations. In Figure 5.21, we have compared two images stego'd with My Secret, the one on the left included a password and the one on the right did not. You noticed that for both images the hidden text begins and ends with a common string. For the image on the left the markers are:

Temp1929479683

And for the image on the right the markers are:

Temp1294555342

The values are actually integer epoch values that can be converted to a readable time value. In the case of 1294555342 above this converts to Sun Jan 09 2011 01:42:22 GMT−0500 (Eastern Standard Time). If found, this can provide additional forensic value.

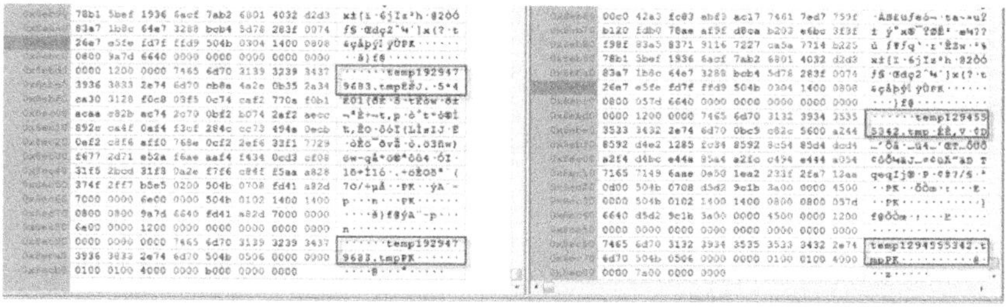

FIGURE 5.21 My Secret Stego Marker Identification

Once again, by combining the data appending detection with the marker alignment we can determine that not only is data hiding confirmed, but My Secret is the likely application that produced the hidden data.

Due to the fact that many of the JPEG-related data hiding activities utilize a data appending method we develop a small python app that will first detect JPEG data appending (as well as, other JPEG structural anomalies) and then extract to the file of your choice. Further analysis of the appended data and most likely brute force decryption would be necessary to recover the plaintext or hidden data. Each data hiding method employs differing privacy or confidentiality measures beyond the original steganography to add yet another dimension the concealment.

STEGDROID

StegoDroid Details	
Application Name	**StegDroid**
Developer/creator	Tom Medley
Carrier format	.ogg Audio
Last release	March 2011

StegDroid is a free application found on the Android market. It was created to compose, and then share, short text messages embedded in audio clips. Since SMS and MMS messages are easy to filter and monitor, the app attempts to cloak such messages in order to avoid detection or filtering. What is most interesting about the application is the use of an audio data hiding method call "echo steganography." The concept is based on earlier work by Jenkins and Martina, among others. Echo steganography, as the name implies, inserts echos such as those that would be normally caused by resonance from walls, windows, desks, computer monitors, keyboards, etc. near the point of recording. These echos are normally ignored by our Human Auditory System (HAS) and our brains. According to tests conducted by Jenkins and Martina (2009), this method meets the imperceptible threshold under most circumstances. In addition, echo steganography has several advantages over other forms of compressed audio embedding:

1. The method can be successful in creating both imperceptible modifications, along with resistance to detection and jamming.
2. The method resists losses typically caused by MP3 compression, creating a more robust method of data hiding.

3. Although the bit rate of embedding is lower than LSB substitution, it performs better than other compressed data hiding methods. Empirical tests have shown a bit rate of 16 bits per second is possible under normal conditions.

Using the Android Application

As soon as the application is opened, the user is instructed to enter a secret text message. The text message has a limit of 120 characters (see Figure 5.22).

Once the message has been typed, the user records audio with the built-in microphone of the Android device. The required length of the audio depends on the length of the text message supplied. The application informs the user when enough audio for successful data hiding has been supplied (see Figure 5.23).

During the echo steganography process two different echo algorithms are used (see Figure 5.24). One algorithm corresponds to a binary "1" and a second corresponds to a binary "0." Thus, depending on what value needs to be hidden (a "0" or "1"), the proper echo algorithm is chosen. When extracting the encoded data, the detection or extraction algorithm attempts to detect the echo and determine the echo type a "1" echo, or a "0" echo, and then records the value. This is repeated until the end of the audio clip. The resulting audio that includes the hidden data is stored in the open container format "ogg." Ogg is typically used to deliver more efficient streaming of multimedia objects (Ogg).

After the embedding is completed, the application then gives the user the choice to decode the message to prove its validity, listen to the recorded message, or send the message via E-mail or other installed applications. When the file is sent, it is transferred as an .ogg attachment. When sending the resulting .ogg file to another user, the accomplice simply needs to obtain the same application and then can recover the hidden message. You may think that detecting or blocking .ogg files would be an easy fix, however, .ogg files are used for a variety of legitimate purposes on Android devices, the most notable is for the exchange of ring tones. Note the application has other modes for privacy and paranoia that allows for encryption of the message prior

FIGURE 5.22 StegDroid Secret Message Entry

to embedding, along with the subsequent deletion of any remnants of the message from the Android device (see Figure 5.25).

We chose to Test Extracting Data and the result is displayed in Figure 5.26.

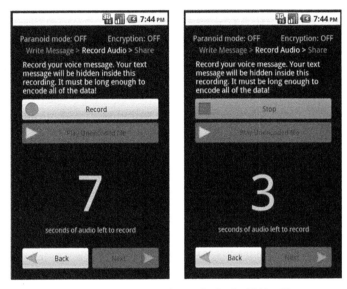

FIGURE 5.23 StegDroid Audio Recording to Create Carrier for Hidden Message

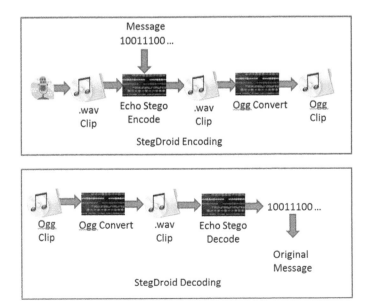

FIGURE 5.24 StegDroid Encoding and Decoding Diagram

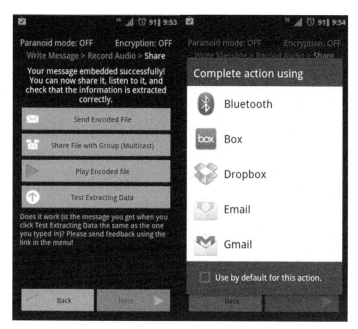

FIGURE 5.25 StegoDroid Send or Review Message

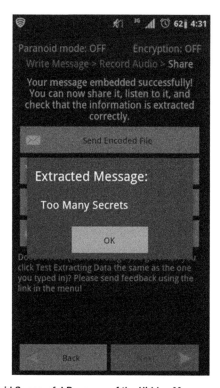

FIGURE 5.26 StegDroid Successful Recovery of the Hidden Message

SUMMARY

Hiding information in video files such as uncompressed AVI and compressed MPEGx is not only possible today, but can provide a significantly sized container that would allow for continuous transmission of hidden data. With current and future innovations in error correction and data redundancy that will allow for the hidden data to survive under even noisy line conditions, streaming of hiding information would certainly enter a new level of threat. The Stego Analyst then has the arduous task of detection or at least jamming these covert channels to prevent against covert communications, exfiltration of intellectual property, or the use of streaming channels for command and control of other malicious code that could accelerate/facilitate advanced persistent threats.

References

Jenkins, N., & Martina, J. E. (2009). Steganography in Audio. Techniques for data hiding. Technical report, University of Cambridge. <http://www.lbd.dcc.ufmg.br/colecoes/sbseg/2009/027.pdf>.

Mauer, U. M. (1990). A universal statistical test for random bit generators. Institute for Theoretical Computer Science, ETH Zürich, CH-8092 Zürich, Switzerland, April 2, 1990 and revised June 23, 1991.

Microsoft, AVI RIFF file reference. <http://msdn.microsoft.com/en-us/library/ms779636.aspx>.

Ogg. The ogg container format. <http://www.xiph.org/ogg>.

## CHAPTER 6

Apple iOS Data Hiding

INFORMATION IN THIS CHAPTER:

- Introduction
- Mobile Device Data Hiding Applications

CONTENTS

INTRODUCTION

The explosion of new data hiding applications for iOS devices, mainly iPad and iPhone has been notable. Whether this is due to the need to improve privacy when using mobile devices, just another venue for app developers to exploit or for more nefarious covert communications purposes is yet to be seen. This chapter takes a detailed look at just three of latest data hiding applications; Spy Pix, InvisiLetter, and Stego Sec. Each of these apps offers a different and unique flavor for data hiding. We examine both the operation and data hiding methodologies employed by these apps.

MOBILE DEVICE DATA HIDING APPLICATIONS

In David Kahn's famous book The Code Breakers, he relays the account of Demaratus who was alleged to have been exiled in Persia. While there, Demaratus learned of a planned attack on Greece by the Persians. As the story goes, Demaratus determined that he must deliver a secret message to the Spartans to warn them. The writing instrument of the day was a wax tablet, as we look at the wax tablet it is quite similar to iPad tablet today, minus the Lithium Ion battery of course (see Figures 6.1 and 6.2).

Demaratus in his day removed the wax from the tablet and then using a sharp object he carved the warning in the wood and then covered the carving with a new coat of wax. This would allow the tablet to make its way through the

107

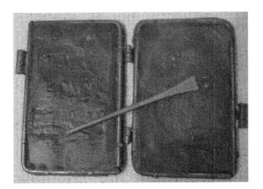

FIGURE 6.1 Wax Tablet

FIGURE 6.2 iPad Writing

guards and sentries of the day and hopefully arrive in time to warn Greece. The tablet eventually reached Cleomenes and he somehow knew to remove the wax and recovered the warning. Having done so, she provided the message to the Spartans allowing them time to prepare and fortify their positions. I wonder if the message will reach the Spartans in time the next time an invasion is imminent (see Figures 6.3 and 6.4).

In addition, unless otherwise noted, we will use the following string when hiding textual data within carrier files: "This is a test of the emergency broadcast system, this is only a test."

FIGURE 6.3 Standard Carrier Image

FIGURE 6.4 Standard Payload Image

For the examples in this chapter we are using an iPad 1 and associated data hiding applications. All apps have been downloaded directly, without modification, from the Apple iTunes site and the iPad has not been Jailbroken or compromised in anyway.

Many data hiding applications exist on the iPhone, iPad, and related devices and in examining the techniques and characteristics of each, we have selected

Spy Pix Details	
Application Name	**Spy Pix**
Seller	Juicy bits
Image format	True color PNG
Last release	December 2009

just a few to include in this chapter that demonstrate unique data hiding techniques. They include:

1. Spy Pix.
2. InvisiLetter.
3. Stego Sec.

Spy Pix Analysis

Like most iPad applications, Spy Pix offers a simple to use application for data hiding. This app employs a hiding method that allows the user to hide a photo within another photo with varying degrees of quality. The resulting data hiding operations reduce the quality of both the carrier and the hidden image, but are still quite difficult to detect.

Once you launch Spy Pix you are presented with the following screen shot (see Figure 6.5).

You must supply two images. The first image is the image you wish to hide (in other words the secret). The second image is the decoy or cover image.

When you select the image to hide selection box, the screen in Figure 6.6 appears.

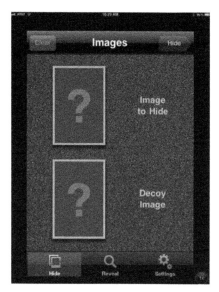

FIGURE 6.5 Spy Pix Image Selection Screenshot

FIGURE 6.6 Spy Pix Photo Source Selection

The application allows the user to either take an immediate picture or to select any existing image from the photo album. We selected the standard gun with bullets image as you can see in the following snapshot (see Figure 6.7).

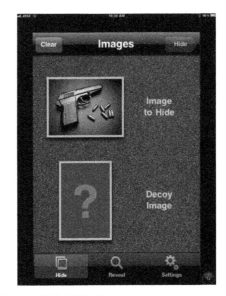

FIGURE 6.7 Spy Pix Gun and Bullet Selection

The process is repeated for the decoy or cover image, shown in the snapshot in Figure 6.8.

At this point, you now can now experiment by combining the two images. The slider at the bottom of the screen, shown in Figure 6.9, provides the user with

FIGURE 6.8 Spy Pix with Selected Hidden and Decoy Image Selected

FIGURE 6.9 Gun and Bullets Bleed Through

the ability to determine the level of hiding that will take place. As you can see in Figures 6.9 and 6.10, by varying the combination selection from low to high you can find the right level. If the level is too low, the photo of the gun and

FIGURE 6.10 Gun and Bullets are Obscured

bullets will bleed through the decoy image, but if you select a higher level, as in Figure 6.10, the decoy successfully obscures the hidden image.

The Spy Pix concept is quite simple—overlay the two images and hide the most significant bits of the image to hide into the least significant bits of the decoy image. Based on how many bits of the hidden picture you wish to preserve, the quality of the resulting image will be reduced.

Data Hiding Method Analysis

Operationally Spy Pix first converts both images to 24 bit true color images in order to normalize the formats. The app then allows the user to specify or experiment with the number of pixels that will be replaced in the cover image— you can choose 0–7 bits. If you choose zero, the entire cover image would be replaced with the hidden image thus destroying the original image. If you were to select seven, only the most significant bit (MSB) of the RGB values of the secret image would replace the least significant bit (LSB) of the cover image.

In Figure 6.11 we selected a data hiding level of 5. This causes bits 7, 6, and 5 of each RGB value of the secret or hidden image to replace the three LSB bits 0, 1, and 2 of the decoy image. As you can see in the illustration, bits 0–4 of the secret image are discarded, thus reducing the resolution of the secret image from 24 bit color image to a 9 bit color image. With 8 bits of color for Red, Green, and Blue = 24, and 5 bits of color removed from each color plane $5 \times 3 = 15$, therefore $24 - 15 = 9$.

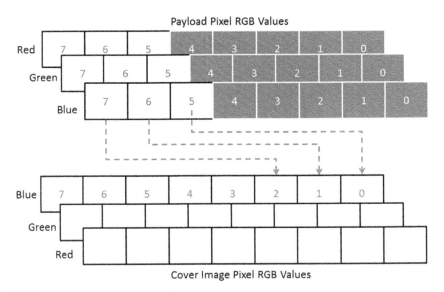

FIGURE 6.11 Spy Pix Data Hiding Diagram

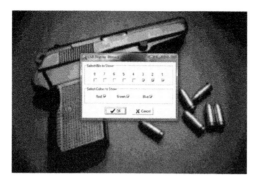

FIGURE 6.12 Stego Analyst LSB Bit Mask Selection

At first glance one might think that this is pretty easy to detect visually. However, by rendering the image it looks quite good even if you replace as many as 2 or 3 bits. In order to reveal the hidden information, we must render the image differently, one method is to render and examine only the LSB values.

We do this by utilizing Stego Analyst, a steganography analysis application by WetStone. Stego Analyst allows the rendering of specific LSB values. See the Snapshot below.

By specifying exactly which bits of the LSB we wish to see and for which colors, we can control the image rendering. In Figure 6.13, we have chosen to display two images side by side. The image on the left is the decoy image with bullets in gun hidden displayed with normal rendering. The image on the right is the same decoy image rendered with only the selected LSB and colors that were specified in Figure 6.12. This gives us the ability to view the images side by side. This reveals the reduced resolution image that was hidden inside the snow owl.

FIGURE 6.13 Side by Side Comparison of the Decoy Rendered Normally (on Left) Rendered with Selected LSB Values (on the Right)

Since only the three MSB values of the secret image were hidden, the data loss is evident, but you can certainly still make out the image of the gun and bullets.

Based on the 9 of 24 bits replaced in the original image, one would think this would be trivial to detect algorithmically. However, the general rule of thumb for LSB detection algorithms is to perform statistical analysis of the LSB values. Many of the predecessors to this approach first compressed then encrypted the desired payload and then modified the LSB values which created randomness in the LSB values of the decoy image. In this case, the data hidden has very little randomization, since the MSB values of the secret image vary much less than even the LSB value of an image, and significantly less than compressed or random data. In order to accommodate this type of detection, new comparison models and neural net training approaches were necessary to detect the anomalies implemented by this simple data hiding method.

The basic approach for developing such a detector is to create a large set of examples using this method along with the original cover images and develop statistical measurements that can distinguish variance within LSB values of "normal" images compared against images that contain variable length replacement of LSB values. The process of training the neural net or other heuristic models is continued until you achieve maximum accurate detection while reducing false positives. For those readers wishing to investigate advanced blind detection methods and neural network approaches, this detail is beyond the scope of this book. However, many good technical papers and resources are available to aid in this scientific research. A good place to start would be research papers by Dr. Jessica Fridrich, http://ws2.binghamton.edu/fridrich/publications.html#Steganography

Stego Sec Analysis

Stego Sec Details	
Application Name	**Stego Sec**
Seller	Raffaele De Lorenzo
Image format	JPEG
Last release	February 2011

The Stego Sec iPhone/iPad app provides the ability to hide text inside a photograph that is either immediately taken or retrieved from previously saved images. The snapshot below reveals the apps navigation panel. We are going to focus our attention on the Crypt Image processing, in other words the creation of the data hiding objects (see Figure 6.14).

As with most mobile apps, Stego Sec allows you to select either images that already exist on your camera roll or you can take an immediate photograph. For consistency, we will select the standard snow owl image that is saved in the camera roll (see Figure 6.15).

The app next prompts us for text that is to be hidden inside the selected image. For this, we typed in the following standard message "This is a test of the emergency broadcast system, this is only a test," a 70 character (byte) message string (see Figure 6.16).

FIGURE 6.14 Stego Sec Application Navigation Panel

FIGURE 6.15 Stego Sec Snow Owl Image Selection

FIGURE 6.16 Stego Sec Hidden Message String

Stego Sec claims to encrypt the text message prior to hiding information in the message. To support this function, we must provide a password. On this same panel we need to supply the file name where the new image will be stored (see Figure 6.17).

FIGURE 6.17 Stego Sec Password and File Name Specification

We confirm by pressing Go and the hidden image is created (see Figure 6.18).

At this point, we can either reveal the hidden message or more importantly send the message to the intended recipient. Stego Sec provides the ability to

FIGURE 6.18 Stego Sec Successful Completion

FIGURE 6.19 Secret Message Distribution

E-mail or MMS the file containing the hidden information (see Figures 6.19 and 6.20).

FIGURE 6.20 Send as E-Mail Selection

FIGURE 6.21 Side by Side Comparison of the Original and Stego'd Image

Data Hiding Method Analysis

As mentioned earlier Stego Sec hides information in a resulting JPEG file type. Since we have all the pieces of the puzzle:

1. The original JPEG image.
2. The JPEG with the hidden content.
3. The message content and length of 70 characters.
4. The password we used to encrypt the data.

We can now interrogate the before and after image and attempt to determine at least the method used to hide the information.

Again we turn to Stego Analyst to assist us in the examination of the resulting images to deduce the hiding methods employed. In Figure 6.21, the image on the left is the original unmodified image of the snow owl. The image on the right is the image created by Stego Sec that contains the hidden emergency broadcast message.

We have labeled this file Stego Sec Hidden Short Message because we will also need to compare messages of differing lengths to confirm the hiding method. In Figure 6.22 we notice is a dramatic difference in the size of the before and after messages:

Original Carrier: 109,562 bytes. Short Hidden Message: 11,525 bytes.

FIGURE 6.22 Stego Analyst Comparison of the Image Details, Short Message vs. Long Message

What we can immediately deduce is that it is likely that hiding method involves re-encoding the JPEG and this further suggests that quantized DCT values inside the JPEG have been altered or there would be no reason to re-encode the image. We have also verified that no stray comment fields, data appending or prepending appears to be present in the JPEG. We have also determined that no other structural anomalies are present. From this we will run another experiment that will help us verify our hypothesis that the hiding method involves altering the quantized DCT values. To assist us with this, we have embedded a second text message using Stego Sec. This one contains a payload length of 350 vs. 70 bytes in the short message and we utilized the same password in order to only modify a single vector (the length of the message).

In Figure 6.23 we compare the two images.

FIGURE 6.23 Quantized DCT Coefficients Comparison, Short vs. Long Messages

Quantized DCT Table Format

	1	2	3	4	5	6	7	8
1	0	1	5	6	14	15	27	28
2	2	4	7	13	16	26	29	42
3	3	8	12	17	25	30	41	43
4	9	11	18	24	31	40	44	53
5	10	19	23	32	39	45	52	54
6	20	22	33	38	46	51	55	60
7	21	34	37	47	50	56	59	61
8	35	36	48	49	57	58	62	63

DC or Average Value

FIGURE 6.24 Quantized DCT Table Showing the DC or Average Value

As you can see the size difference between the Short and Long messages hidden inside the JPEG is quite small:

Long Message Image Size:	11,579
Short Message Image Size:	11,525
A difference of only	54 bytes

However the difference in payload size is $350 - 70 = 280$ bytes. This supports our hypothesis that the hidden data is not simply being added or inserted into non-image areas of the JPEG. In order to more closely examine the changes between the short message and long message data hiding, we will need to directly examine the quantized DCT values of each image, side by side. As you can see in Figure 6.23, the general histogram of the DC coefficients of the quantized DCT appear similar. This is simply displaying the number of occurrences found in the image for each DC value extracted from the quantization table. Figure 6.24 depicts a quantized DCT with what we refer to as the DC coefficient value.

In order to determine the discrete differences between the quantized values, we must take a closer look at a smaller set of individual histogram values. This examination reveals slight changes in the DC values of the coefficient histogram. As you can see in Figure 6.25, the highlighted values represent slight changes in the DC values caused by modification differences between the short and long message strings. Since we started with the same original image, we utilized the same password, and the only change was message length, we can deduce that the hiding method modified DC coefficients with the quantized DCT values. Therefore, the Stego Sec hiding method involves direct modification of the JPEG Lossy values.

Since the message sizes are relatively small (a few hundred bytes), the ability to statistically detect these anomalies without human analysis is quite difficult making Stego Sec a viable data hiding solution for at least small text based messages.

Another very important note regarding Stego Sec, when we originally analyzed the previous version of the app, the hidden data was actually stored in

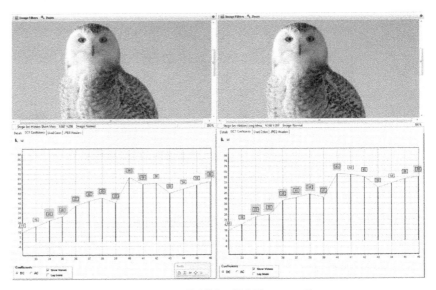

FIGURE 6.25 Short vs. Long Message Highlighted DC Histogram Changes.

a header area of the JPEG making detection and recovery quite simple. Figure 6.26 depicts a hex dumped taken from an image stego'd in the previous version of Stego Sec. The plaintext message in this version was embedded in this version within the EXIF JPEG header.

As we move forward, we expect to see additional updates and improvements to these apps, not only for ease of use, but also for the improvement in the quality of the hiding mechanisms employed.

	0001 0203 0405 0607 0809 0A0B 0C0D 0E0F	0123456789ABCDEF
0x00000	ffd8 ffe1 2ffe 4578 6966 0000 4d4d 002a	ÿØÿá/þExif··MM·*
0x00010	0000 0008 0006 0112 0003 0000 0001 0001	················
0x00020	0000 011a 0005 0000 0001 0000 0056 011b	··············V··
0x00030	0005 0000 0001 0000 005e 0128 0003 0000	·········^·(····
0x00040	0001 0002 0000 0213 0003 0000 0001 0001	················
0x00050	0000 8769 0004 0000 0001 0000 0066 0000	··‡i·········f··
0x00060	00ec 0000 0048 0000 0001 0000 0048 0000	·ì···H·······H··
0x00070	0001 0008 9000 0007 0000 0004 3032 3231	············0221
0x00080	9101 0007 0000 0004 0102 0300 9286 0007	ʻ············ʼ†··
0x00090	0000 0020 0000 00cc a000 0007 0000 0004	··· ···Ì ·······
0x000a0	3031 3030 a001 0003 0000 0001 0001 0000	0100 ···········
0x000b0	a002 0004 0000 0001 0000 0640 a003 0004	···········@ ···
0x000c0	0000 0001 0000 04b0 a406 0003 0000 0001	··········□····
0x000d0	0000 0000 0000 0000 4153 4349 4900 0000	········ASCII···
0x000e0	5468 6973 2069 7320 6120 6869 6464 656e	This is a hidden
0x000f0	206d 6573 7361 6765 0006 0103 0003 0000	message·······
0x00100	0001 0006 0000 011a 0005 0000 0001 0000	········

FIGURE 6.26 Stego Sec Previous Version Simplified Hiding Method

InvisiLetter Analysis

InvisiLetter is yet another interesting application for the iPhone/iPad. The App operates similarly to other iPhone/iPad apps but offers a bit of a twist. As you can see in Figure 6.27, when the app launches you can either embed or extract a secret image.

Our interest, of course, is data hiding so we will choose Embedding Secret Image. Once we do this, the image in Figure 6.28 is displayed and we are prompted first to select a cover image, as shown in Figure 6.29.

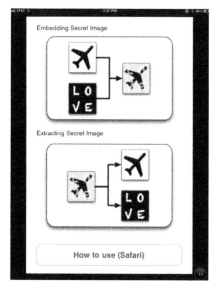

FIGURE 6.27 InvisiLetter App Navigation Panel

InvisiLetter DetailsX	
Application Name	**InvisiLetter**
Seller	Hideaki Tamori
Image format	True color PNG
Last release	July 2010

As you would suspect, you can either take a photo directly with the camera or you can retrieve an image already stored in the Photo Album (see Figure 6.29).

As you can see in Figures 6.30 and 6.31, once you have selected a cover image the app allows you to draw with your finger or other suitable stylus the hidden message directly on the image. For this example, we need to create both a simple message and a slightly more complex message to illustrate the data hiding method.

Data Hiding Method Analysis

The analysis of this method is going to require a slightly different analytic process. Since the resulting image is a PNG image that contains the hidden drawing inside, we would first look at the differences in the two images. As we did when analyzing Stego Sec, we modify only the hidden message. In Figure 6.32 we examine the basics of both the simple drawing (on the left) and the more complex drawing (on the right).

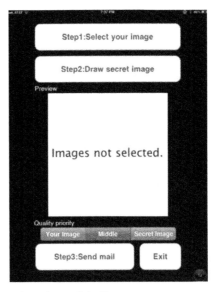

FIGURE 6.28 InvisiLetter Cover Image Selection

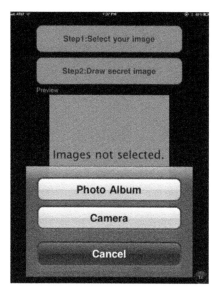

FIGURE 6.29 InvisiLetter Cover Image Selection

At first glance there are two notable differences between the simple and complex images:

1. The file carrying the simple image is smaller in size by 6744 bytes. This is not too surprising when we consider the additional information that needed to

FIGURE 6.30 InvisiLetter Simple Message

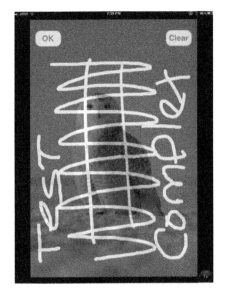

FIGURE 6.31 InvisiLetter Complex Message

FIGURE 6.32 InvisiLetter Simple vs. Complex Embedding

be hidden to record the additional words and drawing elements. The IDAT chunks of PNG images are compressed; however, and any modification to the true color RGB values prior to compression will alter the compressibility.

2. Consistent with the files size increase and more telling are the number of used colors found in the complex image. 55,833 vs. 47,606. Whenever

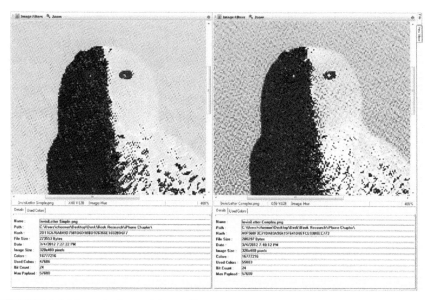

FIGURE 6.33 Stego Analyst InvisiLetter Simple vs. Complex Hue Rendering

we see this type of increase in used colors (for the same carrier image) it implies modification to the LSB values as this modification would increase the number of unique colors found in the uncompressed complex image.

Visually, through normal rendering the images look identical and we don't immediately see any noticeable distortion or artifacts. This image is zoomed at 400% creating some jagged edges, but this is true for the original image, the simple image, and the complex image.

In order to see the difference between the simple and complex images and draw out the changes caused by the data hiding, we need to render the image in a different manner. In Figure 6.33 we have chosen to render the Hue of each image.

The difference is now apparent, as we add more and more hidden data to the image (simple vs. complex) we see the Hue of the image begin to degrade. This is a telltale sign of data hiding that is embedded directly into the RGB values of the image. Examining the image itself, we also verified all the other structural elements have not been modified or altered, thus confirming the embedding is taking place directly into the RGB values of the true color images.

FIGURE 6.34 Snapshot of iPad with Some Popular Data Hiding Apps

SUMMARY

Many data hiding applications currently exist for the iPhone/iPad devices (see Figure 6.34) with many more being created or advanced each day. The rapid development of these capabilities and the broad range of techniques and methods keep many of us up late at night developing new methods to analyze, detect, react, and mitigate the potential harmful effects when used for malicious purposes. This increase and market demand for better ways to conceal and communicate covert information is alarming.

What might this actually imply?

(**A**) People do not feel the built-in encryption features on their devices are sufficient.

(**B**) People don't trust commercial encryption apps.

(**C**) They are more concerned with concealing the existence of the communication vs. the privacy of the data.

(**D**) They want/demand better protection of their personal data .

References

Kahn, D. (1967). *Code breakers.* Scribner. pp. 81–82

Stego Analyst. *A multimedia steganography analysis tool.* WetStone Technologies, Inc. <www.wet-stonetech.com>.

This page is intentionally left blank

## CHAPTER 7

Operating System Data Hiding

INFORMATION IN THIS CHAPTER:

- Windows Data Hiding
- Linux Data Hiding

CONTENTS

With Windows as still the predominant operating system on desktop systems, it's no surprise that it continues to be the most targeted by malicious software. Malware is becoming more complex in a continued effort to evade detection. For example, some malware include functionality that allows a modular approach. This modular approach allows the malware creator to remove certain components while adding other components to the malware, essentially creating a derivative malware. Additionally, the malware may point to another file on an innocuous website such as WordPress. This file may contain C&C (Command and Control) IP addresses. The IP addresses are updated on a regular basis to thwart detection. The malware reaches out to the site to obtain the file, which contains the latest C&C addresses. Furthermore, some of the commands may be embedded in an image file using steganographic techniques. By pasting together multiple techniques, the malware writer can create move evasive software while also modularly swapping out pieces of the functionality on a case-by-case basis. A real-world example of that was Operation Shady RAT (Remote Access Tool).

Operation Shady RAT used a variety of techniques, but the most common involved targeting Windows operating systems using spear-phishing e-mails with a malicious spreadsheet attachment (see Figure 7.1).

The following outlines the attack:

1. The attacker sends e-mails to specific individuals at target institutions (spear phishing).
2. The e-mail contains a seemingly legitimate spreadsheet of contacts.

133

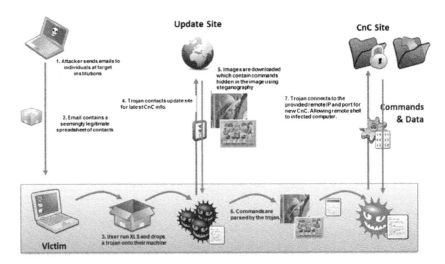

FIGURE 7.1 Operation Shady RAT

3. The user downloads and opens the Excel spreadsheet and unknowingly drops a Trojan onto their machine.
4. The Trojan then contacts an innocuous site (e.g. random Wordpress page) for the latest CnC (command-and-control) information
5. Rather than pulling that information directly from the site, it pulls down image files. These files contain commands hidden in the image files using steganographic techniques.
6. These commands are parsed by the Trojan to reveal the current CnC server information (IP addresses, ports, etc.)
7. The Trojan connects to the provided IP addresses and ports thereby allowing a remote shell into the infected computer.

It was first brought to light by McAfee who revealed a 5-year study at the 2011 Black Hat Conference in Las Vegas.[1] The study was performed from mid-2006 to mid-2011 before publically releasing the report. According to the report, Operation Shady RAT impacted 71 "global companies, governments, and non-profit organizations." These parties included the US Federal Government, United Nations, and Defense Contractors, as well as power and technology companies. In addition, other countries were attacked including Canada, South Korea, Japan, Germany, and many others. Another startling discovery was the length of time these parties were attacked. This ranged from a few months to a few years. Needless to say, the impact was far reaching.

---

[1] Revealed: Operation Shady RAT, McAfee—www.mcafee.com/us/resources/white.../wp-operation-shady-rat.pdf.

Shortly after the McAfee report, Symantec disclosed another layer to the attack not mentioned in the original report.[2] Symantec disclosed more technical details about how Operation Shady RAT was performed and how the CnC server information was stored in image files using steganographic techniques. Since image files are typically allowed to pass through firewalls and intrusion detection systems, the files were easily downloaded by the Trojan to obtain the latest CnC information. By using this technique, it's quite possible that many security products wouldn't have the latest list of CnC servers on the Internet. This approach provides an effective way for the Trojan to stay one step ahead of the CnC detection.

Another case of multidimensional techniques includes the Windows-based Alureon Trojan which also uses steganographic techniques to hide commands with images. These and many other recent attacks demonstrate that hackers are applying multiple techniques to a single piece of malware to enable additional functionality and thwart detection. In this chapter, we explore recent data hiding techniques for Windows systems.

WINDOWS DATA HIDING

Alternate Data Streams Reviewed

Alternate Data Streams in Windows NTFS has been well known for years and dates back to Windows NT 3.1. It was originally designed for interoperability with Macintosh Hierarchical File System (HFS). NTFS uses Alternate Data Streams (ADS) to store metadata related to a file including security information, original author of file, and other metadata.

Alternate Data Streams (ADS) within Windows NT File System (NTFS) is a simple yet effective way to hide carrier files. To the casual investigator a simple directory listing would reveal nothing more than the expected files. Unless anything looked out of the ordinary, the ADS hidden files could remain undiscovered. The following example demonstrates the use of ADS to hide one or more files in the Alternate Data Streams on a Windows machine with NTFS. This provides a simple yet stealthy mechanism for hiding files.

To start, a simple text file is created "mike.txt."

```
D:\mike>notepad mike.txt (Figure 7.2):
```

We can then of course run a directory listing to see the newly created file in our directory:

```
D:\mike>dir
```

---

[2] The truth behind Shady RAT, Symantec—http://www.symantec.com/connect/blogs/truth-behind-shady-rat.

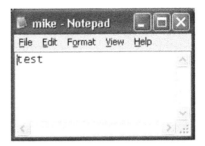

FIGURE 7.2 Creating "mike.txt" in Notepad

```
Volume in drive D has no label.
Volume Serial Number is FFFF-FFFF
Directory of D:\mike
11/07/2005 07:17 PM    <DIR>      .
11/07/2005 07:17 PM    <DIR>      ..
11/07/2005 07:17 PM               4 mike.txt
      1 File(s) 4 bytes
      2 Dir(s) 1,029,111,808 bytes free
```

Next, we can create our first Alternate Data Stream using the original text file (mike.txt) as demonstrated below and in Figure 7.3:

```
D:\mike>notepad mike.txt:mikehidden.txt
```

Normal browsing techniques act as if they're immune to the Alternate Data Streams. Command line or Windows Explorer browsing reveals no new file. Nor has the file size or free space on the disk changed. Even though we've created an alternate data stream "mikehidden.txt" there's no glaring evidence of it:

```
D:\mike>dir
Volume in drive D has no label.
Volume Serial Number is FFFF-FFFF
```

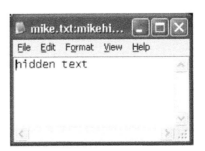

FIGURE 7.3 Creating an Alternate Data Stream

```
Directory of D:\mike
     11/07/2005 07:17 PM      <DIR>      .
     11/07/2005 07:17 PM      <DIR>      ..
     11/07/2005 07:18 PM               4 mike.txt
       1 File(s)             4 bytes
       2 Dir(s)      1,029,111,808 bytes free
```

We're not limited to one Alternate Data Stream per file. Multiple ADSs can be attached to mike.txt (as shown in Figure 7.4):

```
D:\mike>notepad mike.txt:mikehidden2.txt
```

Once again, we can run a directory listing and we see no evidence of either of the Alternate Data Streams:

```
D:\mike>dir
Volume in drive D has no label.
Volume Serial Number is FFFF-FFFF
Directory of D:\mike
     11/07/2005 07:17 PM <DIR>  .
     11/07/2005 07:17 PM <DIR>  ..
     11/07/2005 07:18 PM      4 mike.txt
       1 File(s)      4 bytes
       2 Dir(s)      1,029,111,808 bytes free
```

It also is important to note that most antivirus software packages by default *do not* scan Windows Alternate Data Streams for virus, trojans, and other malicious code. If you're performing forensics investigations, ensure your vendor provides this very important feature its antivirus suite. If it is supported by your antivirus software you can enable this feature on an as-needed basis. The drawback is by leaving this feature on may seriously slow your normal antivirus scans by as much as 10x, which is why many antivirus vendors leave it disabled by default. In summary, Alternate Data Streams are commonly overlooked by investigators and therefore can be a nice hiding location for files.

FIGURE 7.4 Hiding a Second ADS in mike.txt

Stealth Alternate Data Streams

There is a more stealthy way to hide Alternate Data Streams. By attaching an alternate data stream to a reserved device name makes the ADS undetectable with tools such as LDS or streams.exe. Windows includes a number of reserved device names that should not be used as file names. Specifically, the MSDN site lists the following reserved device names: CON, PRN, AUX, NUL, COM1, COM2, COM3, COM4, COM5, COM6, COM7, COM8, COM9, LPT1, LPT2, LPT3, LPT4, LPT5, LPT6, LPT7, LPT8, and LPT9. These reserved device names are intended to send output to hardware peripherals. The key work here is "should" not be used as file names, thereby implying that you could use these reserved device names as file names.

In the following example, we first create a file using the echo command, then perform the same action while attempting to use a reserved device name.

```
C:\sandbox>echo mike > mike.txt
C:\sandbox>echo mike > COM1.txt
The system cannot find the file specified.
C:\sandbox>mkdir COM1
The directory name is invalid.
C:\sandbox>dir
   Volume in drive C has no label.
   Volume Serial Number is AAAA-BBBB
   Directory of C:\sandbox
02/28/2012  03:21 PM          <DIR>                    .
02/28/2012  03:21 PM          <DIR>                    ..
02/28/2012  03:21 PM                        7 mike.txt
             1 File(s)                       7 bytes
             2 Dir(s)        198,873,174,016 bytes free
```

As you can see, attempting to save a file or directory under a reserved device name causes an error. But there is a trick around this limitation.

Since the primary reason to use these reserved device names is for file I/O, we need to avoid the automatic string parsing and send the file unparsed directly to the file system. The \\?\ designation disables string parsing and allows you to send it directly to the filesystem. This is normally used when programming within the Windows API, but we can use it to create files using reserved device names within the filesystem. By combining both a reserved device name and the \\?\ prefix, we can circumvent the standard file parsing and create a file with a reserved device file name.

In this example, we combine the \\?\ option with the reserved device name and create a file called NUL:

```
C:\sandbox>echo mike > \\?\c:\sandbox\NUL
```

A directory list shows the new file called NUL, but native reading of the file fails. This can be helpful if attempting to avoid analysis by some forensic tools or antivirus products.

```
C:\sandbox>dir
     Directory of C:\sandbox
     01/25/2012        09:13 PM           <DIR>            .
     01/25/2012        09:13 PM           <DIR>            ..
     01/25/2012        09:15 PM                        7 NUL
C:\sandbox>more NUL
     Cannot access file \\.\NUL
```

But a user familiar with this technique can still read the contents of the file by simply prepending \\?\ to the command:

```
C:\sandbox>more \\?\c:\sandbox\NUL
   mike
```

Combining this reserved device name technique with Alternate Data Streams creates what someone has coined as a "stealth" alternate data stream.

In order to apply a more stealthy approach, we can combine these reserved device name files with Alternate Data Streams, referred to as "Stealth" Alternate Data Streams. There are a number of advantages to doing this. First, Stealth Alternate Data Streams are not detected by ADS tools such as streams.exe, dir /R, and other techniques. In addition, most tools are not refined enough to detect Stealth ADS. And furthermore, if the ADS is an executable, it can be run using WMIC (Windows Management Instrumentation Command-Line) in conjunction with VBscript, Windows PowerShell, etc. thus allowing an effective way to hide and run malware.

In this example, we attach cmd.exe to CON using an alternate data stream to create our "stealth" alternate data stream.

```
C:\sandbox> type cmd.exe > \\?\c:\sandbox\CON:hiddencmd.exe
```

We can use WMIC to run the previously created cmd.exe executable hidden in the Stealth Alternate Data Stream. This causes a cmd.exe DOS window to pop-up. Although, this executable could have been far more malicious thereby demonstrating that the possibilities are endless (see Figure 7.5).

```
C:\sandbox>wmic process call create
\\.\c:\sandbox\CON:hiddencmd.exe
```

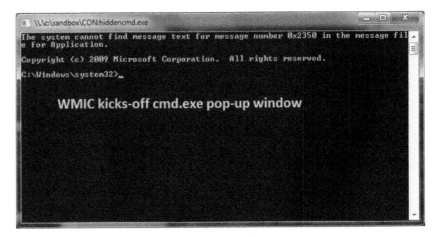

FIGURE 7.5 WMIC Kicking Off a Command Prompt Window

```
Executing (Win32_Process)->Create()
   Method execution successful.
   Out Parameters:
   instance of __PARAMETERS
   {
      ProcessId = 8696;
      ReturnValue = 0;
   };
```

These stealth Alternate Data Streams are typically not detected by antivirus products, even if those products are scanning Alternate Data Streams looking for malware.

Volume Shadowing

Newer versions of Windows, including Vista and Windows 7, include the Volume Shadow Copy Service which backs up disk volumes in case a software install, device driver, or application crash occurs. These snapshots are taken at intervals that vary from system to system depending on system idle points, before software installs, as well as other scenarios. The general rule of thumb is that these snapshots will occur on Vista every 1–2 days, and on Windows 7 every 7–8 days. But keep in mind that software installs and idle times can impact these snapshot intervals.[3]

---

[3] What you should know about volume shadow copy/system restore in Windows 7 and Vista(FAQ)—http://blog.szynalski.com/2009/11/23/volume-shadow-copy-system-restore/.

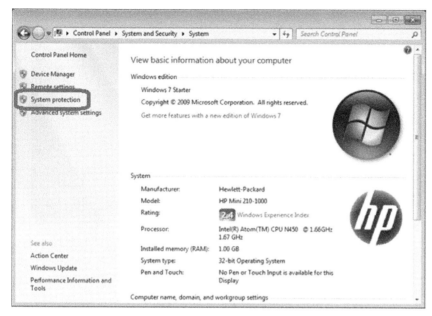

FIGURE 7.6 Access System Protection to View Volume Shadow Copies

Another important note about the Volume Shadow Copy Service is that not every version of a file is stored, say like a VAX/VMS or Mac OS X Lion (10.7) system. In other words, if you're editing a document, not every version is saved, only the version that was saved at the last snapshot interval. In addition, not every file is backed up, only files that have changed. The Volume Shadow Copy Service allocates a fraction of the disk volume or hard drive in which to store these changes. To view the Volume Shadow Copy configuration, go to Control Panel, System, System Protection (see Figure 7.6).

Select System Protection to view the System Properties. The Protection settings will display the pre-existing Shadow Copy volumes. By clicking the Configure button you can also view and modify the storage size. The default maximum size allocated to the Shadow Copy volumes is 15% of the disk volume on Vista and 5% on Windows 7.[4] But the Configure settings allow you to increase the volume to a larger size. Note, only changes are tracked by the Volume Shadow Copies, and only at the snapshot interval, therefore not EVERY change is archived just the differential since the last snapshot. As a result, the Volume Shadow Copy service makes incremental backups, just like server and database

---

[4] How the volume shadow copy service works—http://technet.microsoft.com/en-us/library/cc785914(v=ws.10).aspx.

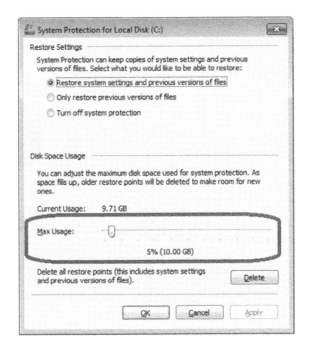

FIGURE 7.7 Shadow Copy Configuration

backups. Thus it's quite possible that multiple snapshots of a file may exist in the Volume Shadow Copy. In addition, Volume Shadow Copies work on a FIFO basis which means that when it runs out of space, the oldest archives are purged to make room for the new ones. It is also important to note that Volume Shadow Copies are read-only (see Figure 7.7).

Now that we have a better understanding about how Volume Shadow Copies works, let's explore this as a potential location for hiding data. Since many antivirus tools do not scan Volume Shadow Copies, it's a great place for hiding data and malware.

The VSSadmin utility provided with Vista and Windows 7 allows the administrator to administer the Volume Shadow Copies from the command line:

```
C:\Windows\system32>vssadmin
---- Commands Supported ----
Delete Shadows          - Delete volume shadow copies
List Providers          - List registered volume shadow copy
                          providers
List Shadows            - List existing volume shadow copies
List ShadowStorage      - List volume shadow copy storage
                          associations
```

```
List Volumes              - List volumes eligible for shadow
                            copies
List Writers              - List subscribed volume shadow copy
                            writers
Resize ShadowStorage      - Resize a volume shadow copy storage
                            association
```

We can view the Shadow Copy volumes and storage sizes by using the "list volumes" option:

```
C:\Windows\system32>vssadmin list volumes
vssadmin 1.1 - Volume Shadow Copy Service administrative command-l
(C) Copyright 2001-2005 Microsoft Corp.
Volume path: \\?\Volume{33faab94-9bc6-11df-9987-806e6f6e6963}\
      Volume name: \\?\Volume{33faab94-9bc6-11df-9987-806e6f6e6963}\
Volume path: C:\
      Volume name: \\?\Volume{33faab95-9bc6-11df-9987-806e6f6e6963}\
Volume path: D:\
      Volume name: \\?\Volume{33faab96-9bc6-11df-9987-806e6f6e6963}\

C:\Windows\system32>vssadmin list shadowstorage
vssadmin 1.1 - Volume Shadow Copy Service administrative command-
   line tool
(C) Copyright 2001-2005 Microsoft Corp.

Shadow Copy Storage association
      For volume: (C:)\\?\Volume{33faab95-9bc6-11df-9987-806e6f6e6963}\
      Shadow Copy Storage volume: (C:)\\?\Volume{33faab95-9bc6-11df-
9987-806e6f6e69
      63}\
      Used Shadow Copy Storage space: 9.707 GB (4%)
      Allocated Shadow Copy Storage space: 9.94 GB (4%)
Maximum Shadow Copy Storage space: 10 GB (4%)
```

The "list shadows" option will allow us to list Volume Shadow Copies, or essentially each of the differential archives at points in time. The last entry is essentially the last archive.

```
C:\Windows\system32> vssadmin list shadows
                 .

                 .

                 .

  Contents of shadow copy set ID: {45540ad8-8945-4cad-9100-
  5b4c9a72bd88}
```

```
Contained 1 shadow copies at creation time: 3/4/2012
5:06:01 PM
        Shadow Copy ID: {670353fe-16ff-4739-ad5e-12b1c09aff00}
            Original Volume: (C:)\\?\Volume{33faab95-9bc6-11df-
9987-806e6f6e6963}\
            Shadow Copy Volume:
\\?\GLOBALROOT\Device\HarddiskVolumeShadowCopy27
            Originating Machine: funhouse
            Service Machine: funhouse
            Provider: 'Microsoft Software Shadow Copy provider 1.0'
            Type: ClientAccessibleWriters
            Attributes: Persistent, Client-accessible, No auto
release, Differential, Auto recovered
```

At this point, we can proceed with creating a file to hide within a Shadow Volume Copy. Then demonstrate that we can access the file independent of the file system. In this example we'll use the cmd.exe executable. We simply copy the cmd.exe to our sandbox lab environment.

```
C:\sandbox>copy c:\windows\system32\cmd.exe .
        1 file(s) copied.


C:\sandbox>dir
  Volume in drive C has no label.
  Volume Serial Number is 98B1-9C5A

  Directory of C:\sandbox
03/06/2012  12:05 PM        <DIR>          .
03/06/2012  12:05 PM        <DIR>          ..
07/13/2009  08:14 PM                301,568 cmd.exe
02/28/2012  03:21 PM                      7 mike.txt
            2 File(s)        301,575 bytes
            2 Dir(s)    199,041,372,160 bytes free
```

Now that we have our file that we'd like to hide in a Shadow Copy Volume, we can now create a new restore point, thereby creating a point-in-time backup that includes our new file. Simply go back to the System Properties tab, and select Create. Then input a name and click create and your shadow copy volume will be archived (see Figures 7.8–7.10).

To confirm that a new Shadow Copy Volume has been created, simply rerun the vssadmin utility to list all of the shadow copies and confirm a new shadow copy volume has been created that is consistent with the time at which you ran the utility.

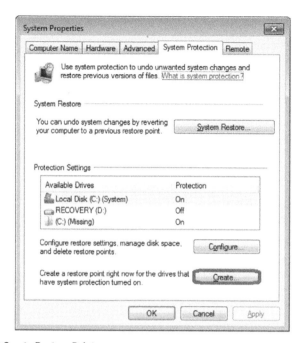

FIGURE 7.8 Create Restore Point

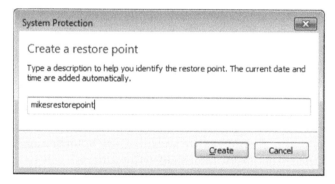

FIGURE 7.9 Creating Shadow Copy Volume

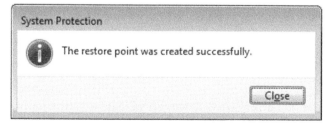

FIGURE 7.10 Shadow Copy Volume (Restore Point) Successfully Created

```
C:\Windows\system32> vssadmin list shadows

                       .

                       .

                       .

   Contents of shadow copy set ID: {85e1aa26-d2d5-4ec5-88c5-
2149b1f1f544}
       Contained 1 shadow copies at creation time: ¾/2012 5:41:00 PM
           Shadow Copy ID: {19e1084c-7965-4092-9bf4-44dc55c1145a}
           Original Volume: (C\\?\Volume{33faab95-9bc6-11df-9987-
806e6f6e6963}\
           Shadow Copy Volume:
   \\?\GLOBALROOT\Device\HarddiskVolumeShadowCopy28
           Originating Machine: funhouse
           Service Machine: funhouse
           Provider: 'Microsoft Software Shadow Copy provider 1.0'
           Type: ClientAccessibleWriters
           Attributes: Persistent, Client-accessible, No auto release,
           Differential, Auto recovered
```

In this case, we can see the addition of a new entry as a result of creating a new restore point. Now that we have created a backup of our volume that contains our hidden executable, we can delete the original executable.

```
C:\sandbox> del cmd.exe
```

At this point, the file only exists in the shadow copy volume, and arguably on the disk drive if performing low-level forensics and it hasn't been overwritten. We can now view the contents of the Shadow Copy Volume by creating a symbolic link to it. To do this we need to review the output of our "vssadmin list shadows" and make note of the Shadow Copy Volume name: "\\?\GLO-BALROOT\Device\HarddiskVolumeShadowCopy28." We will run the mklink command using the /D option to create a directory for the symbolic link. Note that we also append a "\" to the end of the Shadow Copy Volume name, a prerequisite for creating the symbolic link.

```
C:\sandbox>mklink /D hiddendirectory
    \\?\GLOBALROOT\Device\HarddiskVolumeShadowCopy28\
    symbolic link created for hiddendirectory <←=>>
    \\?\GLOBALROOT\Device\Harddisk
    VolumeShadowCopy28\
```

Once the symbolic link is created, we can validate this by simply performing a directly listing of the directory and we can now see our "hiddendirectory" symbolic link.

```
C:\sandbox>dir
   Volume in drive C has no label.
   Volume Serial Number is 98B1-9C5A

   Directory of C:\sandbox

   03/04/.2012  05:52 PM    <DIR>            .
   03/04/2012   05:52 PM    <DIR>            ..
   03/04/2012   05:52 PM    <SYMLINKD>       hiddendirectory
   [\\?\GLOBALROOT\Device\Ha
   rddiskVolumeShadowCopy28\]
   02/28/2012   03:21 PM        7 mike.txt
                1 File(s)        7 bytes
             3 Dir(s)   199,002,898,432 bytes free
```

We can review contents of the Shadow Copy Volume through the symbolic link by changing to the hiddendirectory and performing a directory listing. Additionally, we can confirm the "cmd.exe" executable we planted by viewing that directory and confirming that it exists in the shadow copy volume.

```
C:\sandbox>cd hiddendirectory
C:\sandbox\hiddendirectory>dir
   Directory of C:\sandbox\hiddendirectory
11/10/2010  10:01 PM                         1,024.rnd
06/10/2009  04:42 PM                         24 autoexec.bat
03/04/2012  05:19 PM    <DIR>                book
06/10/2009  04:42 PM                         10 config.sys
02/13/2012  04:38 PM    <DIR>                HP Universal Print Driver
03/04/2012  05:29 PM    <DIR>                myprogram
02/24/2012  02:45 PM              56,384 offreg.dll
07/13/2009  09:37 PM    <DIR>                PerfLogs
07/29/2011  02:31 PM    <DIR>                Personal
10/21/2010  10:17 AM    <DIR>                Pre
04/14/2011  10:10 PM    <DIR>                Program Files
03/04/2012  05:39 PM    <DIR>                sandbox
07/30/2010  02:11 PM    <DIR>                SwSetup
01/31/2011  11:31 AM    <DIR>                temp
02/24/2012  02:40 PM             784,896 tsk-xview.exe
12/14/2010  02:58 PM    <DIR>                Users
10/01/2011  11:27 PM    <DIR>                Windows
             5 File(s)     842,338 bytes
```

```
            14 Dir(s)  199,031,443,456 bytes free
C:\sandbox\hiddendirectory>cd sandbox
C:\sandbox\hiddendirectory\sandbox>dir
   Volume in drive C has no label.
   Volume Serial Number is 98B1-9C5A
   Directory of C:\sandbox\hiddendirectory\sandbox
03/04/2012  05:39 PM    <DIR>          .
03/04/2012  05:39 PM    <DIR>          ..
07/13/2009  08:14 PM           301,568 cmd.exe
02/28/2012  03:21 PM                 7 mike.txt
             2 File(s)        301,575 bytes
             2 Dir(s)  199,031,443,456 bytes free
```

Since our objective was to simply confirm the existence of the "cmd.exe" file we hid in the Shadow Copy Volume, we can now go back and remove the symbolic link by removing the "hiddendirectory."

```
C:\sandbox>rmdir hiddendirectory
```

At this point, we're now ready to demonstrate that the "cmd.exe" file is accessible and executable, but not viewable from the filesystem. We can do this by using the WMIC utility to run the executable. It is important to note that when using WMIC, that a "." should be used instead of a "?"

```
C:\sandbox>wmic process call create
\\.\GLOBALROOT\Device\HarddiskVolumeShadowco
py28\sandbox\cmd.exe
Executing (Win32_Process)->Create()
Method execution successful.
Out Parameters:
instance of __PARAMETERS
{
      ProcessId = 5780;
      ReturnValue = 0;
};
```

Running the WMIC command successfully kicks off the hidden executable (cmd.exe) and a command window pops-up (Figure 7.11).

Bring this altogether we can see that Volume Shadow Copies can be used to hide files. If the file is an executable, WMIC can be used to execute the program from a Volume Shadow Copy without the need for a symbolic link to the

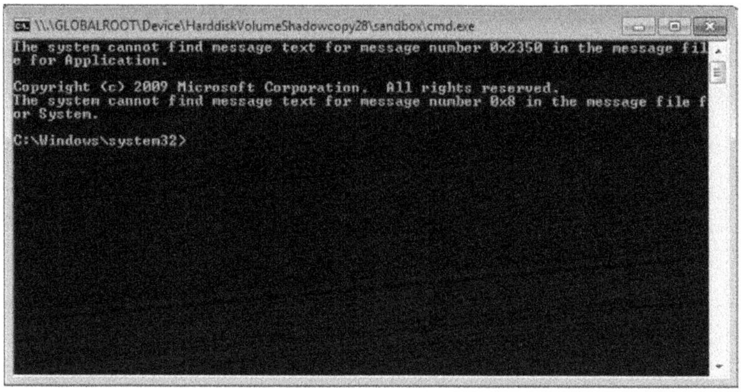

FIGURE 7.11 WMIC Command Kicking Off a Hidden Executable (cmd.exe)

file. In addition, most antivirus and antimalware products don't scan Volume Shadow Copies. This is a great place to hide files, malware, and other artifacts. It is important to note that Volume Shadow Copies are not permanent and they will eventually be purged to make room for newer restore points. But for the standard PC this could easily be 6 months or longer, leaving plenty of time for malware to perform its damage.

Tim Tomes and Mark Baggett released a tool at Hack3rCon II called vssown. vbs that allows you to view and manipulate the volume shadow copies.[5] This allows you to create or delete volume shadow copies.

```
c:\sandbox>cscript vssown.vbs
Microsoft (R) Windows Script Host Version 5.8
Copyright (C) Microsoft Corporation. All rights reserved.
Usage: cscript vssown.vbs [option]
  Options:
  /list                       - List current volume shadow
  copies.
  /start                      - Start the shadow copy service.
  /stop                       - Halt the shadow copy service.
  /status                     - Show status of shadow copy
  service.
  /mode                       - Display the shadow copy service
  start mode.
  /mode [Manual|Automatic|Disabled] - Change the shadow copy service
  start mode.
```

---

[5] Hack3rCon II—Lurking in the shadows, Tim Tomes & Mark Baggett—http://www.youtube.com/watch?v=ant3ir9cRME.

```
/create                          - Create a shadow copy.
/delete [id|*]                   - Delete a specified or all shadow
copies.
/mount [path] [device_object]    - Mount a shadow copy to the given
path.
/execute [\path\to\file]         - Launch executable from within an
unmounted shadow copy.
/store                           - Display storage statistics.
/size [bytes]                    - Set drive space reserved for
shadow copies.
/build [filename]                - Print pasteable script to stdout.
```

What's important is that it can be also run using a remote shell script and execute a command in a shadow copy. This code bundled with malware would be very stealthy and difficult to detect on an infected host.

LINUX DATA HIDING

With the proliferation of Linux and the open source movement, Linux's scalability, availability, and acceptance in the server community had bled over into the user community. As a result, Linux is commonly found on many desktops and laptops, and now numerous mobile devices. This represents arguably limitless possibilities for hiding data. Let's explore some examples of data hiding in Linux.

Linux Filename Trickery

There are some rudimentary ways to hide files and directories in Linux. For example, it is commonly known to Linux users that putting a dot "." at the beginning of a file name will allow one to hide a file within a directory. But this is really only hidden from the "ls" command and can be easily revealed using the "ls –al" command:

```
spihuntr@spihuntrubuntu:~/sandbox2$ vi .mike.txt
spihuntr@spihuntrubuntu:~/sandbox2$ ls
spihuntr@spihuntrubuntu:~/sandbox2$ ls -al
total 12
drwxr-xr-x  2 spihuntr spihuntr      4096 2012-06-01 00:10  .
drwxr-xr-x 44 spihuntr spihuntr      4096 2012-06-01 00:10  ..
-rw-r--r--  1 spihuntr spihuntr        15 2012-06-01 00:10 .mike.txt
```

The directory listing also reveals a single dot and a double dot. The single dot is the current directory, and the double dot is the parent directory.

What's interesting is that you can add spaces to the dot to create a new directory, for example a dot space ". ".

```
spihuntr@spihuntrubuntu:~/sandbox2$ mkdir      ". "
spihuntr@spihuntrubuntu:~/sandbox2$ ls -al
total 16
drwxr-xr-x 3 spihuntr spihuntr 4096 2012-06-01 00:11 .
drwxr-xr-x 2 spihuntr spihuntr 4096 2012-06-01 00:11 .
drwxr-xr-x 44 spihuntr spihuntr 4096 2012-06-01 00:10 ..
-rw-r--r-- 1 spihuntr spihuntr 15 2012-06-01 00:10 .mike.txt
```

To most users the second single dot would probably be overlooked. It's almost as if this directory is hiding in plain sight. The same can be performed for the ".." representative of the parent directory. You can use dot dot space ".. " to create a second hidden directory as well.

```
spihuntr@spihuntrubuntu:~/sandbox2$ mkdir ".. "
spihuntr@spihuntrubuntu:~/sandbox2$ ls -al
total 20
drwxr-xr-x 4 spihuntr spihuntr 4096 2012-06-01 00:11 .
drwxr-xr-x 2 spihuntr spihuntr 4096 2012-06-01 00:11 .
drwxr-xr-x 44 spihuntr spihuntr 4096 2012-06-01 00:10 ..
drwxr-xr-x 2 spihuntr spihuntr 4096 2012-06-01 00:11 ..
-rw-r--r-- 1 spihuntr spihuntr 15 2012-06-01 00:10 .mike.txt
```

These duplicate dots show no indication of the spaces. Most casual and experienced users would overlook this and not recognize that some of the dots are actual directories containing additional hidden files. These make for a very simple hiding place for files. This trick can be performed on many distributions of Linux including Ubuntu, Mac OS, and Android.

Extended Filesystem Data Hiding

Extended filesystems (ext2, ext3, and ext4) are found within many Linux distributions ranging from Ubuntu to Mac OS to Android. Additionally, these filesystems (as well as other Linux and Unix filesystems) contain inodes. Every file or directory is represented by an inode. Each inode contains information about the file type, access rights, owners, timestamps, size, and pointers to data blocks.[6]

In Extended filesystems, when a file is deleted, the filesystem removes the file-name to inode association, but the file data is not deleted until overwritten

---

[6] Design and implementation of second extended file system. http://e2fsprogs.souceforge.net/ext2intro.html.

when the filesystem needs space for a new file. The inode stores the deletion time when the file is deleted. Bottomline, unless the file data is overwritten, the inode maintains everything except for the filename. Therefore the data can be recovered in many cases, but this hinges largely upon how active the filesystem is. If attempting this on a very active server, the chances of recovering this data are less than an inactive extended filesystem, such as one found on a thumb drive.[7]

If we apply this knowledge of extended filesystems and inodes, we can use this to hide files and recover them by saving them in an inode. Linux recovery tools exist for recovering these "nameless" files from their inodes. "debugfs" is a recovery tool found in many Linux distributions, but can be a bit cumbersome for non-Linux savvy individuals. Fortunately, Oliver Diedrich created a simpler Linux tool called "e2undel."[8]

Let's begin by first creating a thumb drive with an extended filesystem so we can create a way to hide data. In this example, we'll use Ubuntu. There are a number of partitioning tools in Linux, but we'll use GParted in this scenario. If Gparted is not bundled with your Linux distribution, you can download it from Sourceforge at http://gparted.sourceforge.net.[9] To start, simply run "gparted" from the command line to start the GParted GUI (Figure 7.12).

Next, from the dropdown at the right, choose the thumb drive you'd like to format. As with any formatting, ensure that you have the right drive so you don't format your main operating system by accident. If the device is mounted simply right-click on the device and select "unmount" from the menu. Then select format and choose "ext2" (Figure 7.13).

Then follow the prompts to kick-off the formatting process (see Figure 7.14).

When the format is complete, the new partition will be labeled "ext2" (see Figure 7.15).

Now that we have our ext2 filesystem, we can start hiding some data. Our methodology involves copying or creating files on our thumb drive, then deleting them (or hiding them). If we want to recover the deleted or hidden files at a later time, we can use the "e2undel" tool. Referencing the main page:

```
e2undel -d device -s path [-a] [-t]
with
-d device: the file system where to look for deleted files (like /dev/
hda1)
```

---

[7] Deleted files recover howto—http://e2undel.sourceforge.net/recovery-howto.html.

[8] E2undel—http://e2undel.sourceforge.net/.

[9] Gparted—http://gparted.sourceforge.net/.

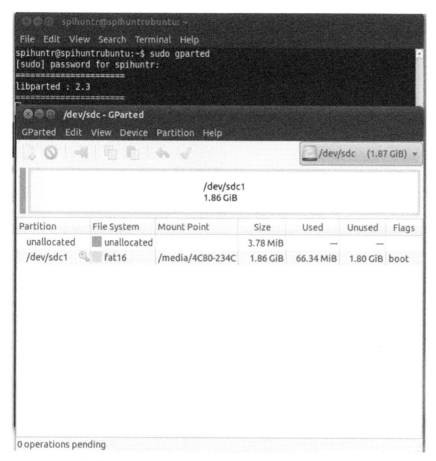

FIGURE 7.12 Running GParted to Partition the Thumb Drive

```
-s path: the directory where to save recovered files
-a: work on all files, not only on those listed in undel log file
(you need this if you don't use the undel library or want to recover a
file that was deleted prior to installing libundel)
-t: try to determine type of deleted files without names, works only
with '-a'
```

In our example, we will recover the two files we previously deleted. We define the device (-d) and path to the destination where we can save the recovered files (-s).

```
spihuntr@spihuntrubuntu:~$ sudo e2undel -d /dev/sdc1 -s
  /home/spihuntr/sandbox -a -t
```

FIGURE 7.13 Format Thumb Drive as ext2

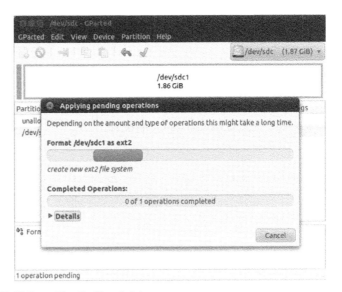

FIGURE 7.14 Formatting the Thumb Drive

```
e2undel 0.82
Trying to recover files on /dev/sdc1, saving them on
  /home/spihuntr/sandbox
```

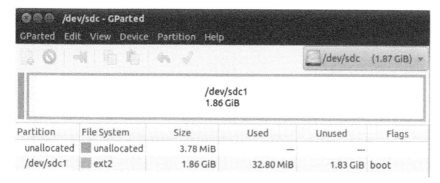

FIGURE 7.15 The Formatted Thumb Drive with ext2 Filesystem

```
/dev/sdc1 opened for read-only access
/dev/sdc1 was not cleanly unmounted.
Do you want to continue (y/n)? y
122160 inodes (122149 free)
487992 blocks of 4096 bytes (479595 free)
last mounted on Wed Dec 31 19:00:00 1969
/dev/sdc1 is mounted. Do you want to continue (y/n)? y
reading log file: opening log file: No such file or directory
no entries for /dev/sdc1 in log file
searching for deleted inodes on /dev/sdc1:
|======================================================|
122160 inodes scanned, 2 deleted files found
   user name | 1 <12 h | 2 <48 h | 3 <7 d | 4 <30 d | 5 <1 y | 6 older
-------------+---------+---------+-------+---------+--------+--------
spihuntr     |      2 |      0 |     0 |      0 |      0 |     0
```

First we are prompted for the username. As mentioned earlier, the inode saves the deletion time. "e2undel" uses this to provide a table of deleted files broken out by timeframes. Therefore, at the second prompt we enter our timeframe of less than 12 h by entering a 1 at the prompt.

```
Select user name from table or press enter to exit: spihuntr
Select time interval (1 to 6) or press enter to exit: 1
   inode     size   deleted at          name
-----------------------------------------------------------
     12        15   May 31 14:31 2012   * ASCII text
     13        27   May 31 14:32 2012   * data
```

This will now display details about each of the files to be recovered. Since we're going to recover both files, we select inodes 12 and 13. Then hit enter at the file prompt to exit.

```
Select an inode listed above or press enter to go back: 12
15 bytes written to /home/spihuntr/sandbox/inode-12-ASCII_text
Select an inode listed above or press enter to go back: 13
27 bytes written to /home/spihuntr/sandbox/inode-13-data
Select an inode listed above or press enter to go back:
   user name | 1 <12 h | 2 <48 h | 3 <7 d | 4 <30 d | 5 <1 y | 6 older
-------------+---------+--------+--------+---------+--------+--------
    spihuntr |       2 |      0 |      0 |       0 |      0 |      0
Select user name from table or press enter to exit:
spihuntr@spihuntrubuntu:~$
```

Our files should now be saved in our destination directory. By changing to the destination directory, we can see our saved inodes as files. Since the filename is lost when the file is deleted, the recovery automatically assigns a filename to the recovered file.

```
spihuntr@spihuntrubuntu:~/sandbox$ ls -al
total 32
drwxr-xr-x 2 spihuntr spihuntr 4096 2012-05-30 22:21 .
drwxr-xr-x 2 spihuntr spihuntr 4096 2012-05-30 22:23 ..
-rwxr-xr-x 1 root     root       15 2012-05-31 14:33 inode-12-
   ASCII_text
-rwxr-xr-x 1 root     root       27 2012-05-31 14:33 inode-13-data
```

Now is the moment of truth. We originally hid our files in our extended filesystem by deleting them. Then we used "e2undel" to recover the files. If we review the contents of the file, we can see it contains the data from the original file.

```
spihuntr@spihuntrubuntu:~/sandbox$ more inode-12-ASCII_text
hidden message
spihuntr@spihuntrubuntu:~/sandbox$
```

Our tactic was a success! These techniques are not limited to just ext2 extended filesystem. "debugfs" for example can be used to recover files in ext3 and ext4 filesystems as well. In addition, although we performed this on a Ubuntu distribution, this technique would work on Mac OS, Red Hat, Android, and other distributions that use extended filesystems. But it should be noted that the technique is not completely foolproof. Very active extended filesystems will overwrite their deleted files far more often, this minimizing life of the deleted file before it's overwritten. But for a personal laptop, with a spare partition, or for hiding data on a thumb drive this technique is very useful and every effective.

TrueCrypt

Per the TrueCrypt[10] website "TrueCrypt is a software system for establishing and maintaining an on-the-fly-encrypted volume (data storage device). On-the-fly encryption means that data is automatically encrypted right before it is saved and decrypted right after it is loaded, without any user intervention. No data stored on an encrypted volume can be read (decrypted) without using the correct password/keyfile(s) or correct encryption keys. Entire file system is encrypted (e.g. file names, folder names, contents of every file, free space, meta data, etc.)."

TrueCrypt also provides the means to create a "hidden" volume. To some, this provides "plausible deniability" when confronted by an adversary. Plausible deniability is a situation in which there is "little or no evidence of wrongdoing or abuse." In legal terms, "it refers to the lack of evidence proving an allegation." Providing a way to hide volumes allows users to arguably employ plausible deniability of confronted by an adversary to reveal suspected evidence. TrueCrypt's design does not contain known file headers and the data when analyzed appears as pure random data.

A real-life case involved TrueCrypt and plausible deniability.[11] Daniel Dantas was a banker suspected by the Brazilian government of financial crimes. The Brazilian police confiscated five hard drives secured using TrueCrypt. After 5 months of analysis, the Brazilian National Institute of Criminology deferred the analysis to the FBI, but after an addition 12 months the FBI was also unsuccessful with cracking them.[12]

TrueCrypt has captured worldwide attention and is worthy of a deeper view into how this tool works. Let's explore TrueCrypt with a walkthrough, of the installation and use of the product. TrueCrypt is supported on a number of platforms including Windows and Linux. In this walkthrough, we have downloaded the gzip from the TrueCrypt website truecrypt.org (see Figures 7.16 and 7.17).

---

[10] TrueCrypt—www.truecrypt.org.
[11] Schneier, B. (2006). Plausible deniability—Definition within the context TrueCrypt Schneier on security, a blog converting security and security technology, Blog April 18—http://www.schneier.com/blog/archives/2006/04/deniable_file_s.html.
[12] Brazilian banker's crypto baffles FBI—http://www.theregister.co.uk/2010/06/28/brazil_banker_crypto_lock_out/.

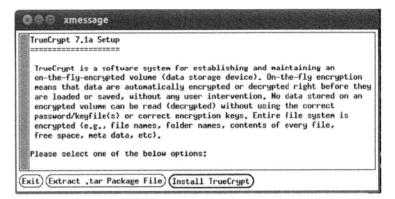

FIGURE 7.16 TrueCrypt Setup

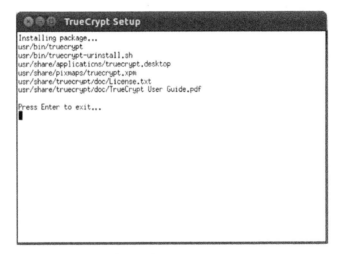

FIGURE 7.17 TrueCrypt Package Installation

Once installed, the GUI can be initiated from the Linux prompt by simply running "truecrypt":

```
spihuntr@spihuntrubuntu:~$ truecrypt
```

In this walkthrough we're going to use a 2GB USB thumb drive to create a TrueCrypt drive with a hidden volume. For this we plug-in our USB drive into our Ubuntu laptop and select the "Create a volume with a partition/drive." Then choose "Hidden Volume" (see Figures 7.18 and 7.19).

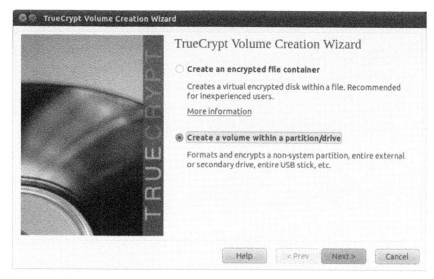

FIGURE 7.18 Choosing a Partition/Drive for Our Hidden Volume

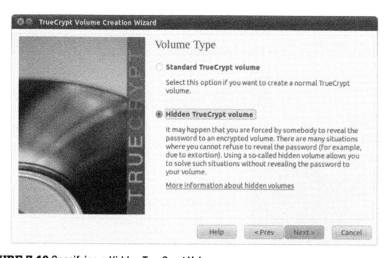

FIGURE 7.19 Specifying a Hidden TrueCrypt Volume

This will prompt for a partition or device. In this example, we choose our 2GB thumb drive and then our encryption options (see Figures 7.20–7.22).

Next, the Volume Creation Wizard will format the "Outer Volume." This will be the host volume for one or more hidden volumes (see Figure 7.23).

FIGURE 7.20 Choosing the Thumb Drive for the Hidden Volume

FIGURE 7.21 Choosing AES as the Volume Encryption

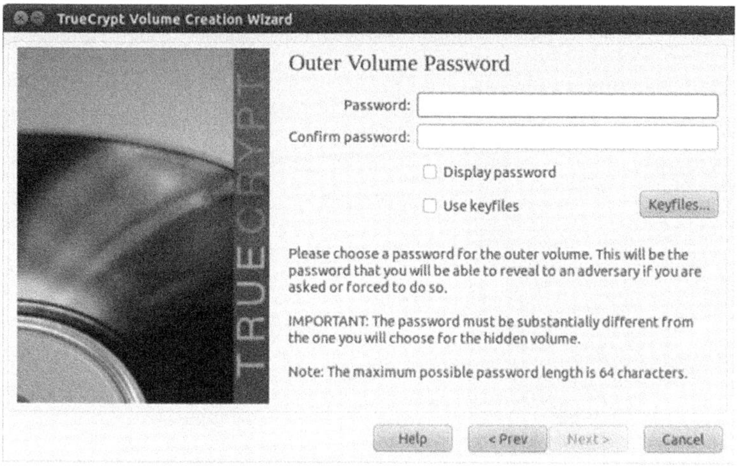

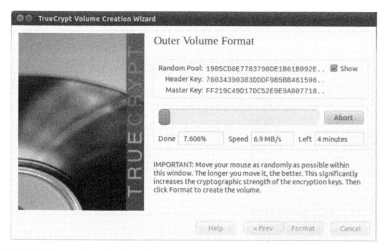

FIGURE 7.22 Choosing a Password for the "host" Volume

FIGURE 7.23 Formatting the "host" Volume

Once installed, the GUI can be initiated from the Linux prompt by simply running "truecrypt." Then the program will walk you through the "Hidden Volume" setup (see Figures 7.24–7.27).

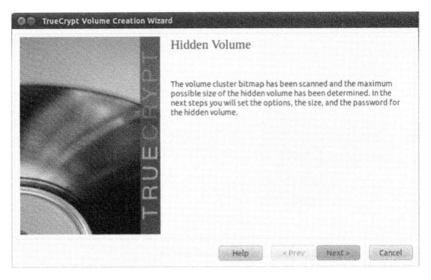

FIGURE 7.24 TrueCrypt "Payload" Volume Creation Wizard

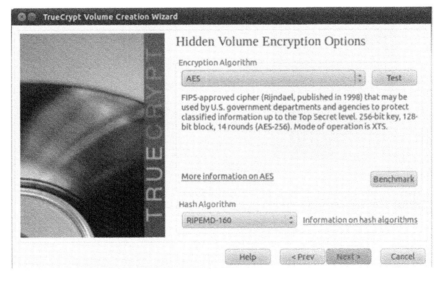

FIGURE 7.25 "Payload" Hidden Volume Encryption Options

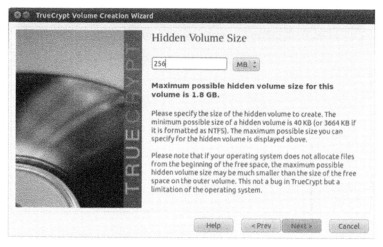

FIGURE 7.26 "Payload" Hidden Volume Size Option

FIGURE 7.27 "Payload" Filesystem Type

Once complete, we can now mount and open our hidden volume. Choose the "Select Device" to choose our 2GB USB thumb drive (see Figure 7.28).

This will prompt you for the password used during the setup and will then allow the volume to be mounted (see Figure 7.29).

FIGURE 7.28 Mounting and Opening Newly Created Volume

FIGURE 7.29 Entering Password Used During Setup to Protect the TrueCrypt Volume

Viewing the properties allows you to review the details about the TrueCrypt volume including the encryption (see Figures 7.30 and 7.31).

FIGURE 7.30 Viewing the TrueCrypt Volume Properties

The volume is now fully accessible until unmounted. As demonstrated, the setup for TrueCrypt is straightforward when using the wizard. This level of encryption, randomization of data, and ability to hide data in volumes is quite powerful. This also runs under Windows, putting the power of this program in the hands of virtually anyone. A forensic investigator would be quite challenged in even determining if a drive has TrueCrypt encrypted data on it, and recovery of this without the password is nearly impossible as of the publication of this book.

It is important to note that Peter Kleissner demonstrated at Black Hat USA 2009 that his Stoned bootkit can circumvent TrueCrypt's MBR (Master Boot Record) thus bypassing the full volume encryption.[13] But this only works in specific circumstances. Specifically, the user running an untrusted executable bootkit with root privileges, and secondly allowing physical access to the drive.[14] In other words, if you're going to use TrueCrypt follow security best practices.

---

[13] Stoned bootkit—http://www.blackhat.com/presentations/bh-usa-09/KLEISSNER/BHUSA09-Kleissner-StonedBootkit-PAPER.pdf.
[14] TrueCrypt vs. Peter Kleissner, or Stoned BootKit revisited—http://ctogonewild.com/2009/08/04/truecrypt-vs-peter-kleissner-or-stoned-bootkit-revisited/.

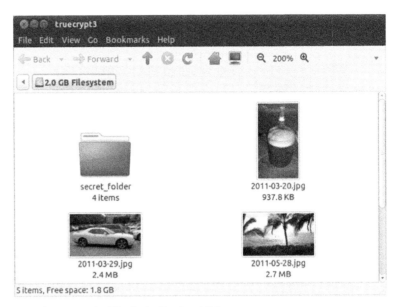

FIGURE 7.31 Access the Files in the TrueCrypt Volume

References

Brazilian banker's crypto baffles FBI. <http://www.theregister.co.uk/2010/06/28/brazil_banker_crypto_lock_out/>.

Deleted files recover howto. <http://e2undel.sourceforge.net/recovery-howto.html>.

Design and implementation of second extended filesystem. <http://e2fsprogs.sourceforge.net/ext2intro.html>.

e2undel. <http://e2undel.sourceforge.net/>.

Gparted. <http://gparted.sourceforge.net/>.

Hack3rCon II – Lurking in the shadows. <http://www.youtube.com/watch?v=ant3ir9cRME>.

How the volume shadow copy service works. <http://technet.microsoft.com/en-us/library/cc785914(v=ws.10).aspx>.

Revealed: Operation Shady RAT. <www.mcafee.com/us/resources/white.../wp-operation-shady-rat.pdf>.

Schneier, B. (2006). Plausible deniability – Definition within the context TrueCrypt Schneier on security, a blog covering security and security technology, Blog April 18. Stable URL: <http://www.schneier.com/blog/archives/2006/04/deniable_file_s.html>.

Stoned bootkit. <http://www.blackhat.com/presentations/bh-usa-09/KLEISSNER/BHUSA09-Kleissner-StonedBootkit-PAPER.pdf>.

The truth behind Shady RAT. <http://www.symantec.com/connect/blogs/truth-behind-shady-rat>.

TrueCrypt. <www.truecrypt.org>.

TrueCrypt vs. Peter Kleissner, or Stoned BootKit revisited. <http://ctogonewild.com/2009/08/04/truecrypt-vs-peter-kleissner-or-stoned-bootkit-revisited/>.

What you should know about volume shadow copy/system restore in Windows 7 & Vista (FAQ). <http://blog.szynalski.com/2009/11/23/volume-shadow-copy-system-restore/>.

## CHAPTER 8

Virtual Data Hiding

INFORMATION IN THIS CHAPTER:

- Introduction
- Hiding a Virtual Environment
- A Review of Virtual Machines

CONTENTS

INTRODUCTION

Corporations continue to enforce stricter rules and requirements on end user computers to deter infection by malware, viruses, Trojans, and undesired use. With the proliferation of virtual machines or virtual environments, users are becoming craftier in finding ways to use these virtual machines to access programs and Websites blocked by their company. In addition, malicious users are also using virtual machines to remain anonymous while stealing corporate secrets or confidential data such as PII (personal identifiable information) or credit card information.

Detecting these virtual environments across the enterprise network remains an ongoing challenge for administrators. These virtual environments can elude detection by anti-virus, network scans, and end-point protection, as many of these products do not scan virtual machines. To further complicate the detection problem, some of these virtual machines can run from removable storage such as USB drives or SD cards. For example, a portable version of VirtualBox is available which allows one to run VirtualBox on a USB thumb drive. Other virtual environment products are specifically designed to be carried from computer to computer, such as MojoPac.

Data Hiding. http://dx.doi.org/10.1016/B978-1-59-749743-5.00008-0

HIDING A VIRTUAL ENVIRONMENT

MojoPac by RingCube was acquired by Citrix and is still available in a free version from http://www.mojopac.com. MojoPac allows you to run a virtual environment on a USB thumb drive and carry it from computer to computer, thus allowing you to carry your specifically tuned Windows XP environment from computer to computer. But aside from the arguable shortcoming, its ease of setup and portability makes it very attractive to anyone looking to hide a virtual environment on their desktop.

Getting Started

To get started simply download the latest version of MojoPac from the Website. You will also need a USB thumb drive, preferably a new one with no data on it. MojoPac is essentially going to treat the drive like a standard Windows C:\ drive (see Figure 8.1).

Once you kick-off the installation, the next screen will ask you to pick the target drive, in this case your USB drive. Note that there is also an "Add shortcut to desktop" option. If your goal is to hide your tracks, it would be a good idea to disable this before proceeding (see Figure 8.2).

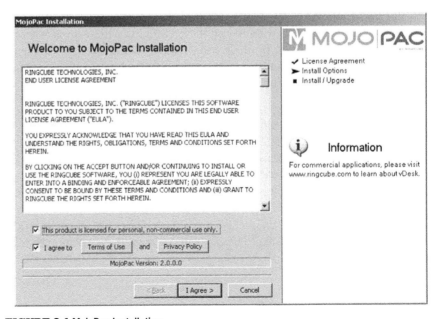

FIGURE 8.1 MojoPac Installation

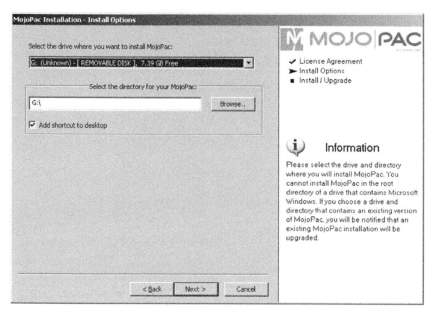

FIGURE 8.2 MojoPac Drive Selection

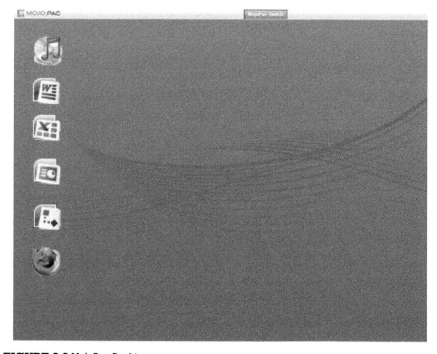

FIGURE 8.3 MojoPac Desktop

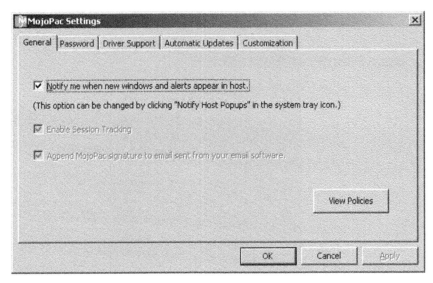

FIGURE 8.4 MojoPac General Tab

The installation program will then proceed to prepare the drive for the virtual machine. Following the installation, you can now run the MojoPac desktop (see Figure 8.3).

The MojoPac USB drive can now be carried from Windows XP machine to Windows XP machine, thereby allowing the user to attempt to avoid detection.

It should be noted that remnants of MojoPac's use on a Windows XP machine may remain following its use. As detailed in Barrett's "Virtualization and Forensics,"[1] evidence of MojoPac's use can be found on the host system in the ntuser.dat, prefetch files, the page file, and other documented places. Some of this is configurable in the professional version of MojoPac. By going to the General Tab, you can click on Policies (within Settings in the General tab) to configure (or limit) the interaction between the host machine and the MojoPac virtual environment (see Figures 8.4 and 8.5).

With these settings you can limit access to the fixed and removable drives on the PC, disable access to the MojoPac filesystem from the host, among other settings. These options can be used to thwart detection over the network or with a host-based IDS.

---

[1] Virtualization and Forensics, by Barrett.

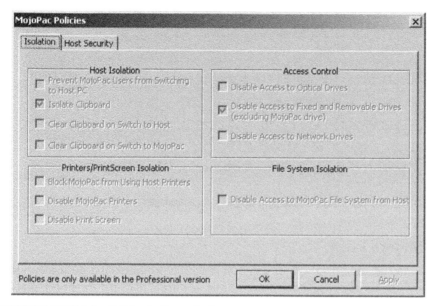

FIGURE 8.5 MojoPac Policies for Rogue Settings

A REVIEW OF VIRTUAL ENVIRONMENTS

In the previous section, we review MojoPac, a virtual environment that runs within the host operating system. There are also a number of virtual machine products the most common of course being VMware. These virtual machine products contain an entire operating system.

Typically when hiding large chunks of data, multimedia files are commonly used due to their large size. As described in earlier chapters, spreading that hidden data across a 100 MB multimedia file has minimal effect on the multimedia file itself, yet allows for larger quantities of data to be hidden when compared to say a 2 MB JPEG file. The result is a multimedia file whose video or sound quality is typically unaffected. But if a large quantity of data, say 2 MB is hidden within a JPEG file, the result is easily seen since the image will typically become very fuzzy or fragmented.

Due to their large size, virtual machines also make a great place to hide large quantities of data. But unlike static multimedia files, virtual machines dynamically change in size on an ongoing basis when the virtual machine is in use. This circumvents traditional data integrity programs that seek to identify illegitimate changes to a file. Therefore, in order to hide data within a virtual machine, we must first understand the components of a virtual machine.

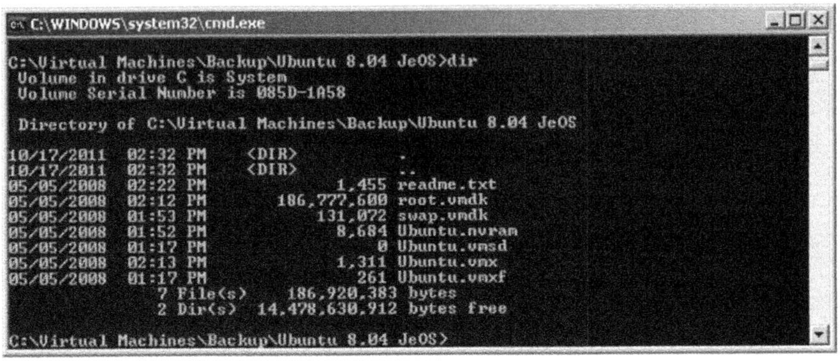

```
C:\WINDOWS\system32\cmd.exe
C:\Virtual Machines\Backup\Ubuntu 8.04 JeOS>dir
 Volume in drive C is System
 Volume Serial Number is 085D-1A58

 Directory of C:\Virtual Machines\Backup\Ubuntu 8.04 JeOS

10/17/2011  02:32 PM    <DIR>          .
10/17/2011  02:32 PM    <DIR>          ..
05/05/2008  02:22 PM             1,455 readme.txt
05/05/2008  02:12 PM       186,777,600 root.vmdk
05/05/2008  01:53 PM           131,072 swap.vmdk
05/05/2008  01:52 PM             8,684 Ubuntu.nvram
05/05/2008  01:17 PM                 0 Ubuntu.vmsd
05/05/2008  02:13 PM             1,311 Ubuntu.vmx
05/05/2008  01:17 PM               261 Ubuntu.vmxf
               7 File(s)    186,920,383 bytes
               2 Dir(s)  14,478,630,912 bytes free

C:\Virtual Machines\Backup\Ubuntu 8.04 JeOS>
```

FIGURE 8.6 Sample File Listing for a VMware Virtual Machine

VMware Files

In order to hide data within a virtual machine, we must first understand the components of a virtual machine. A VMware virtual machine image is typically comprised of a small group of files. There is a page on the VMware site titled "What Files Make Up a Virtual Machine?"[2] at VMware.com that lists the files and their purpose (see Figure 8.6).

*.vmdk—This file is the virtual hard drive. These files can be a maximum of 2 GB in size. In addition, the *.vmdk file contains the virtual machine's data, plus space for overhead. *.vmdk files were formally known as *.dsk in older versions of VMware.

*.nvram—Virtual machine's BIOS and the number of hard drives.

*.vmsd—Used to store the state of the virtual machine by taking a snapshot and storing the snapshot metadata.

*.vmx—A text file that stores the configuration of the virtual machine. It stores information about the operating system, devices, network interfaces, etc. Below is an example of a *.vmx configuration file (see Figure 8.7).

*.vmxf—Additional file that contains the metadata for virtual machines operating as a team.

Hiding Data in a VMware Image

Now that we have an understanding of the files that comprise a VMware image, we can now focus on the appropriate carrier file for the larger file we'd like to hide. Since the virtual hard drive *.vmdk is really the only large file, we'll focus

[2] What files make up a virtual machine? http://www.vmware.com/support/ws55/doc/ws_learning_files_in_a_vm.html.

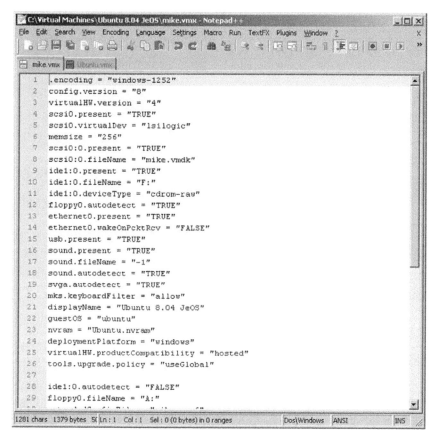

FIGURE 8.7 *.vmx VMware Configuration File Contents

on that. The files can range from 50 MB to 2 GB. And in enterprise environments they can range into the terabytes range. But the reality is that for our use, a reasonable file size for download or transfer over the network is ideal, so a 50 MB file is more ideal.

If you don't have a *.vmdk file to use, there are hundreds of virtual appliances available for free on the VMware site. Simply download your favorite appliance and you will receive a bundle that includes all of the files necessary for running your virtual machine. Included you will find the virtual disk file *.vmdk. Note that you will also need to download VMware Player from the VMware site if you don't have that already (see Figure 8.8).

Before we begin with hiding our data in the *.vmdk file, we must ensure that the virtual machine is shutdown and not running. Otherwise it could have

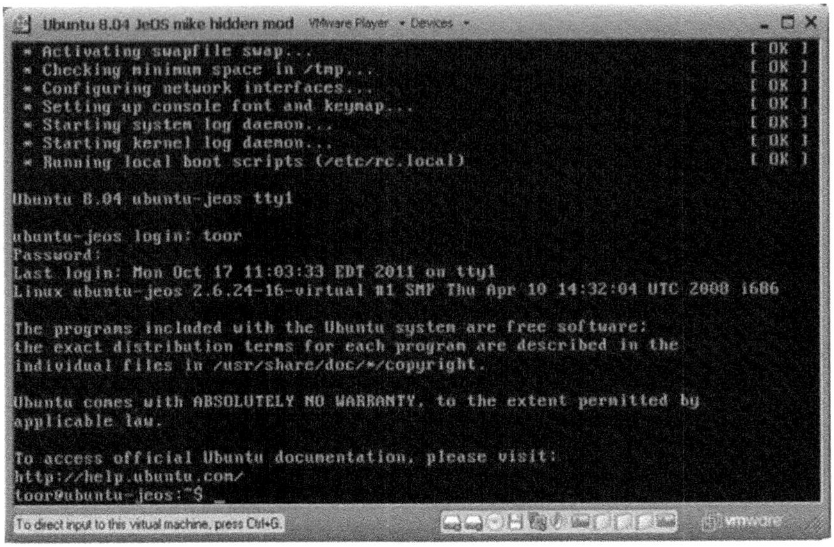

FIGURE 8.8 Running the Ubuntu 8.04 Virtual Machine Downloaded from VMware.com

adverse effects. If the virtual machine is shutdown, we can then open the *.vmdk file within WinHex for analysis to determine the best hiding location for our payload.

Headers for *.vmdk files can vary, but the most common is KDMV (vmdk spelled backwards) found in monolithicSparse files. MonolithicSparse files are essentially virtual disks that are all one file. Also contained with the *.vmdk file is a descriptor file that details the disk layout, geometry (similar to a physical disk geometry), and size of the virtual image as well as where it exists on the disk (as signified by the offset). Bottomline, it is important to keep the size of the *.vmdk the same to ensure there are no inconsistency errors when the virtual machine is run.

In addition, since a *.vmdk file is essentially a virtualized version of the physical hard disk, it contains padding just like the padding in the partitions and sectors of a physical hard drive. As a result, you will find lots of padding scattered throughout the virtual disk, especially towards the end of the file (see Figure 8.9).

For our example, we'll use a 2 MB JPEG file and insert it into the virtual disk *.vmdk. Rather than append it to the file, we will actually replace a 2 MB chunk of padding and data with the contents of the 2 MB file. We could accomplish this using WinHex to simply copy our payload file over to the *.vmdk file and use WinHex's replace functionality replace the bytes. But there is a VMDK file editing tool we can use to accomplish the same task.

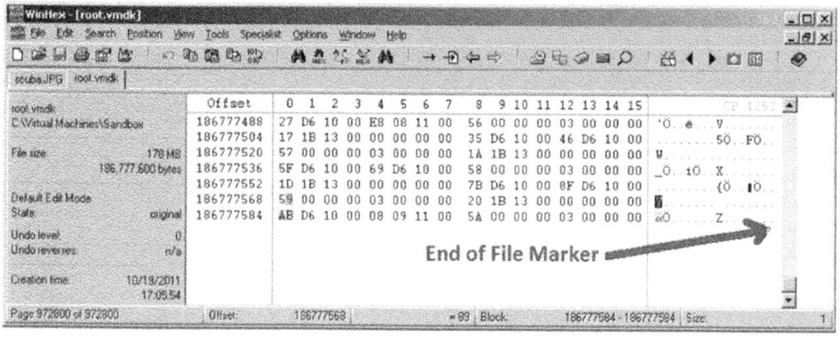

FIGURE 8.9 Random Padding Within the Virtual Disk Represented by the Zeros

Dsfok-tools (sanbarrow.com)[3] is a group of programs for Windows designed to edit VMDK files without the need to open the VMDK file in a hex editor. Normally the tools are used to edit the descriptor file contained within the VMDK file. Included in the toolset are dsfo and dsfi. The dsfo program allows configuration information to be extracted from the VMDK file, whereas dsfi can be used to inject data into the VMDK file. Since we'd like to insert our JPEG payload file into the VMDK carrier file, we can use the dsfi to modify the existing bytes, rather than appending it to the file, rather than changing the size of the VMDK file which could corrupt it. In addition, changing the VMDK file size could cause errors at runtime because it would also make the file size inconsistent with the descriptor file size parameter.

Per sunbarrow.com, dsfi uses the following syntax:

```
dsfi <destination> <offset> <size> <source>
```

- Null size is interpreted as max possible input.
- Negative size is calculated on current file size.
- Negative offset is calculated from end of file.
- Use "e" as offset to indicate end of file.
- Use "$" as destination to check MD5 signature only.

Our goal is to start with the EOF marker and go backwards far enough to allow us to insert our JPEG payload file. In order to do this we need to determine the size of the JPEG file. If we open the file in WinHex, we can determine the raw file size in the left-hand column. We determine this to be 1,571,228 bytes (see Figure 8.10).

---

[3] dskfok-tools http://sanbarrow.com.

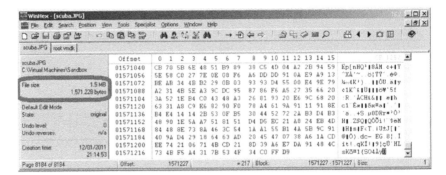

FIGURE 8.10 JPEG Payload File Size

FIGURE 8.11 Using dsfi Tool to Insert Payload File into VMDK Carrier File

We can now use dsfi to insert the JPEG file into the *.vmdk file. We can use the negative offset to calculate from the end of the file. If root.vmdk is our file name, our command would then be (see Figure 8.11):

```
C:\ dsfi root.vmdk -1571228 1571228 scuba.jpg
```

If we now reopen the root.vmdk file in WinHex, we can see the JPEG file was inserted by replacing the last 1,571,228 bytes of the root.vmdk file with the contents of the JPEG file (see Figure 8.12).

We now have a virtual disk *.vmdk file with an image embedded within it. This could be left as a dead drop on the network to be picked up by the recipient at a later time.

The interesting thing is that VMDK file will still play within VMware Player, and it still operates like a normal virtual machine, which has no indication that it's been tampered with. There are no alerts to the user, not even a prompt asking if you would like to copy or move this image before playing it, as is common with new images that have been downloaded. Nor is there a message that the virtual machine has been modified since last use. If a before and after

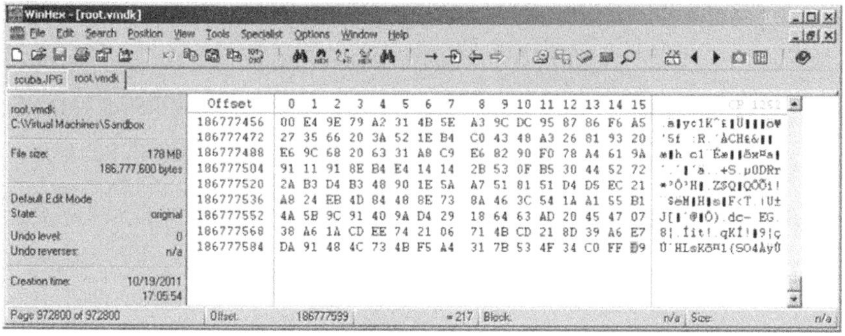

FIGURE 8.12 JPEG Inserted into root.vmdk

image existed, they could be compared in a hex editor to identify the insertion of the JPEG file.

Simply playing the virtual machine over and over has no impact on the hidden picture. But since we're talking about a virtual disk, this hidden data will probably be written over with other disk data if the virtual machine is used frequently. The reality is that in a dead drop scenario, the intended user can simply use the virtual disk as a covert carrier mechanism. The intended user has no concern if others download the virtual machine, play it, and eventually unknowingly overwrite the hidden data. In fact, that may actually be a plus! In the example below, the virtual machine is run following the insertion with no impact on the virtual machine's functionality (see Figure 8.13).

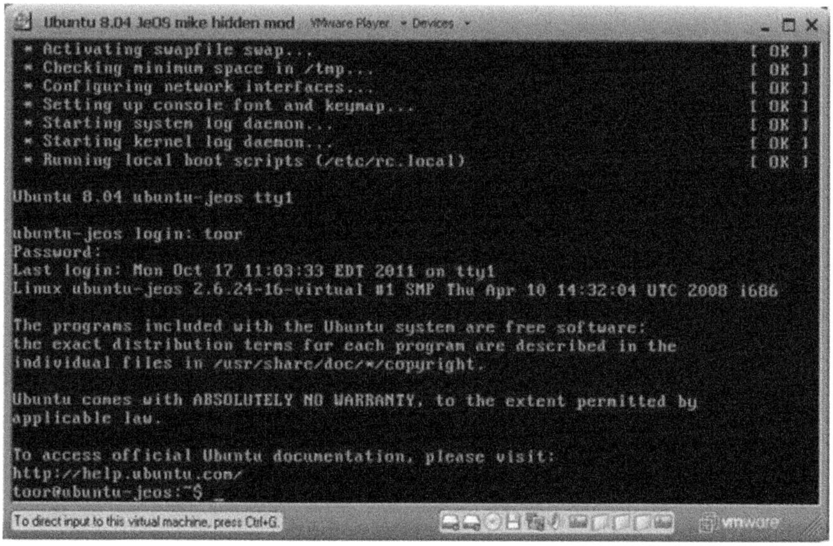

FIGURE 8.13 VMware Virtual Machine Running Cleanly Following Insertion of JPEG

Extracting the hidden picture from the VMware virtual machine vmdk file is very similar to hiding it (see Figure 8.14).

For this we can use the other tool bundled with aforementioned dsfok-tools called dsfo:

C:\ dsfo root.vmdk -1571228 1571228 scuba.jpg

This will extract the last 1,571,228 bytes of the file and store it in "scuba.jpg."

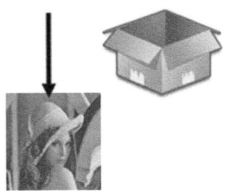

FIGURE 8.14 Extract Picture from VM

SUMMARY

In this chapter we've demonstrated ways to hide virtual environments and techniques for hiding data within a virtual machine. Although these techniques may be less common than others demonstrated in this book, they are very viable and also stealthy in nature. The use of virtual environments to hide data must be given serious consideration when deploying a security strategy to detect and deter undesirable use on the network. For those with large virtual machine deployments, data integrity of these systems should be given serious consideration.

References

Barrett, D., & Kipper, G. (2010). *Virtualization and forensics*. Syngress Publishing. (pp. 58–61)

dsfok-tools. <http://sanbarrow.com/vmdk-tools.html#dsfo>.

What files make up a virtual machine? <http://www.vmware.com/support/ws55/doc/ws_learning_files_in_a_vm.html>.

This page is intentionally left blank

## CHAPTER 9

Data Hiding in Network Protocols

INFORMATION IN THIS CHAPTER:

- Introduction
- VoIP Data Hiding
- Delayed Packet Modification Method
- IP Layer Data Hiding, The TTL Field
- Investigating Protocol Data Hiding

CONTENTS

INTRODUCTION

On Cinco de Mayo in 1997, which happened to be the first Monday in May that year, the hacker publication *First Monday* included an article entitled, "Covert Channels in the TCP/IP Protocol Suite," by Rowland.

"The TCP/IP protocol suite has a number of weaknesses that allow an attacker to leverage techniques in the form of covert channels to surreptitiously pass data in otherwise benign packets. This paper attempts to illustrate these weaknesses in both theoretical and practical examples" (Rowland, 1997).

The methods employed in this paper exposed data hiding vulnerabilities in the Transmission Control Protocol (TCP) and demonstrated a very simple and straightforward method for hiding data in the TCP initial handshake sequence. In some ways, this served as a warning that hiding information within a data stream was not only plausible but was also simple and practical. As with most cyber security related warnings of this type, there was an initial outcry to develop more secure protocols that could mitigate such threats. Once the voices died down, we moved on to the next threat of the day and many forgot about the vulnerability.

In order to illustrate the real flexibility in Covert TCP we modified Craig's original work and utilized the initial sequence number for data hiding. Let's take a

181

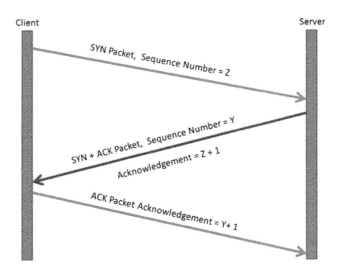

FIGURE 9.1 Covert TCP Initial Handshake Sequence

closer look at the Covert TCP approach. Figure 9.1 shows a typical TCP three way handshake necessary to make a TCP connection. When setting up a connection, the critical element of our modified Covert TCP is the selection of the initial sequence number.

Since the initiator of the session (in this example the client) specifies the initial sequence number we have what we need, a way to convey information through the control of the sequence number. In the Wireshark snapshot shown in Figure 9.2 we have highlighted the client-specified sequence number both as the decimal value converted by Wireshark and the hex value in the TCP Packet at the bottom. Actually, we need to examine the hex value and convert it to decimal properly interpreting it as a small endian value:

C4 52 0B 00 → 00 0B 52 C4 hex when converted from little endian

This hex value interpreted yields a decimal value of 742,084 (0B 52 C4 converted hex to decimal).

To obscure the information being hidden for this simple example we chose to use a constant multiplier K that would be shared between the client and server of 6236. Thus whatever single byte value we wish to send we multiply that ASCII value by the arbitrary constant 6236:

ASCII value $\times$ K = Sequence Number

Then to recover the hidden characters on the server side you reverse the process:

Sequence Number K = ASCII value

For the example in Figure 9.2, we were attempting to transmit the letter "w" which is 119 in decimal. To do so we follow the formula state above:

$119 \times 6236 = 742{,}084$ Decimal $= 00$ 0B 52 C4 in hex

The execution of the complete message transferred is shown in Figure 9.3.

We could improve on this technique by becoming more sophisticated with the cover, using for example XOR value to cover the string of characters we wish to transmit, and this would also then improve randomness of the each successive sequence number. This data hiding or leakage method is limited to sending 1 or 2 bytes per connection, but if you need to exchange keys, short messages, or just provide a beacon this method would be hidden in the haystack of billions of connects made each day from even small organizations.

I wonder if a viable solution will exist by Monday May 5, 2014 when Cinco de Mayo falls once again on the first Monday in May? As of today, not only is the TCP protocol still vulnerable to Craig's initial warning, but hundreds of new protocols have arrived on the scene, most containing a plethora of opportunities to hide information in innocuous ways.

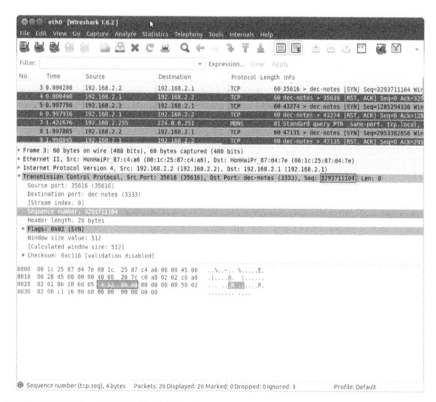

FIGURE 9.2 Wireshark TCP Handshake Capture

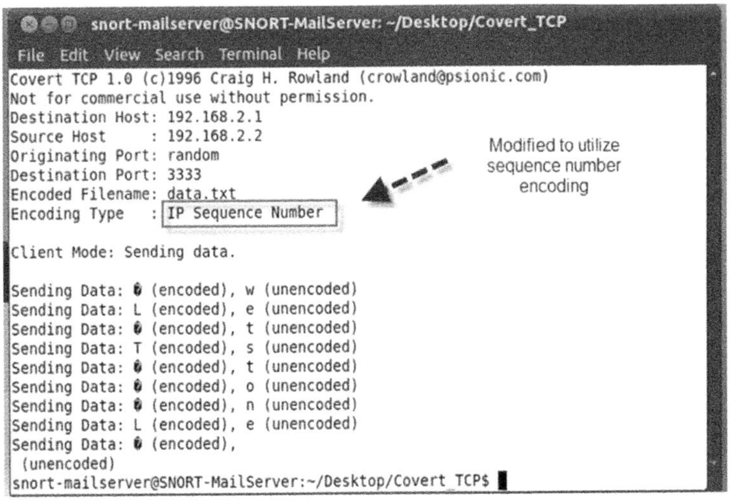

FIGURE 9.3 Covert TCP Execution with Modified Sequence Number Method

VOIP DATA HIDING

One of the new areas of interest is Voice over Internet Protocol (VoIP) solutions. The reasons are quite obvious: VoIP is ubiquitously deployed and utilized; VoIP solutions generate a large number of small packets which would be ideally suited for hiding small pieces of a larger message; and finally, the wide variety of packet types, codecs, and encoding methods for VoIP abound, providing cover for the needle in a haystack.

VoIP utilizes network transport mechanisms that are inherently unreliable. The underlying Real-Time Transfer Protocol (RTP) and the Universal Datagram Protocol (UDP) do not retransmit lost or delayed packets. At first glance this would appear to be a huge drawback for data hiding activities, since losing packets that contain portions of the secret message—especially if they were encrypted—would be problematic. Actually, one of the methods we will discuss leverages this weakness into a strength.

To begin, I'm going to focus on a simple RTP protocol running on top of UDP in a point-to-point arrangement to explain the core elements of the data hiding method. Of course to execute this within a true VoIP setting, you would need to work with session initiation protocol (SIP), Real-Time Transfer Control Protocol (RTCP) and others. The diagram below depicts this simplified structure.

Figure 9.4 depicts a simplified version of the VoIP RTP packet structure. As you can see, the RTP packet is a payload of the UDP packet which carries out the unreliable transport. In turn, the UDP packet is the payload of the IP packet,

VoIP RTP Packet Structure

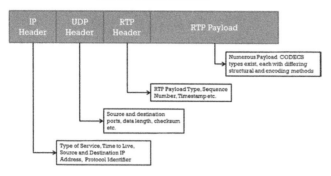

FIGURE 9.4 VoIP RTP Simplified Packet Overview

which provides the Internet routing needed. In Figure 9.5 we turn our attention then to the RTP packet exchange between the now infamous Alice and Bob.

As you can see in Figure 9.5, Alice and Bob exchange a sequence of RTP packets in a continuous stream. As you recall from above, packets can be missing, dropped, out of sequence, or delayed, but since the protocol is not meant to be completely reliable, data continues to stream. As mentioned, control packets and other protocol elements that can assist in re-establishing connections if things go bad have been omitted from this 30,000 ft view.

The simplest method of data hiding available is to insert content directly into the payload section of each packet. The secret message is broken up into small chunks and embedded directly into the payload. The current methods we have evaluated uses one of the two basic schemes: (see Figure 9.6)

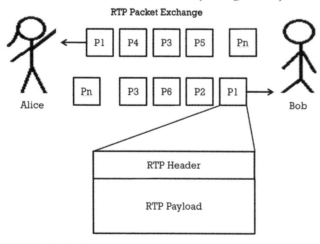

FIGURE 9.5 RTP Packet Exchange Alice and Bob

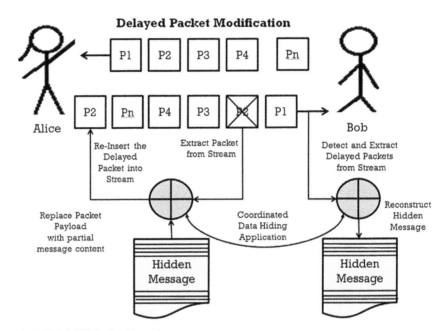

FIGURE 9.6 RTP Payload Insertions

1. The small chunks of the overall secret message are inserted into the header of the payload section of the RTP packet. Since most RTP payload types have a built-in header that provides information to the receiver about the configuration of the payload, it is possible to insert a small number of bytes into this payload header.
2. The small chunks of the secret message are broken into a bit stream and each bit is used to overwrite the least significant bit of encoded data within the payload.

As you can see in Figure 9.7, we have performed a capture during a RTP VoIP session between two hosts. We have highlighted one packet of 1000s streaming between two local hosts 192.168.2.1 and 192.168.2.2. In order to make the data hiding visible we inserted a small test phrase into the payload of the RTP packet namely "Data Hiding." Normally this would either be encrypted content or broken into a bit stream that would be embedded in the LSB of content of the payload to make it virtually invisible. Thus in the myriad of packets streaming between the hosts, discovery would be difficult at best.

The problem with both methods of course is that if data loss occurs (lost or delayed packets), some of the hidden data will also be lost. This can be overcome by transmitting redundant packets (secret message chunks). The applications

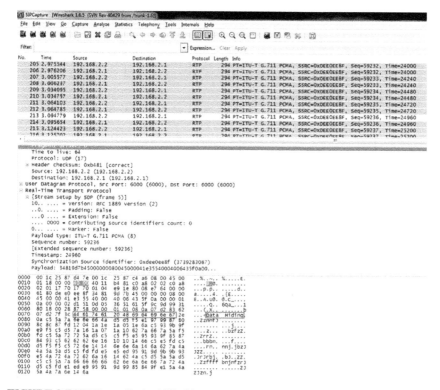

FIGURE 9.7 RTP Theora Payload Hijacking

we have reviewed that perform this function allows for the setting of both the redundancy and frequency of the retransmission.

DELAYED PACKET MODIFICATION METHOD

The next method I reviewed is actually the most interesting, and is depicted in Figure 9.8. This method actually takes advantage of the fact that RTP packets are sometimes delayed, delivered out of order, or lost in transmission as a core element of the spoof. This approach systematically extracts specific packets from the data stream before they are released by the sender. This causes certain packets to purposely not be delivered in a timely fashion to the receiver. The receiving application, whether VoIP or an audio player, automatically compensates for the delayed packet and fills in the blanks, if you will. Since most RTP packets only contain a few milliseconds of audio, the compensation is hardly ever noticed when listening to a conversation or even a streamed audio track.

Here is the best part! Once the packet has been extracted from the stream, the data hiding application can utilize the full payload section to insert slices of

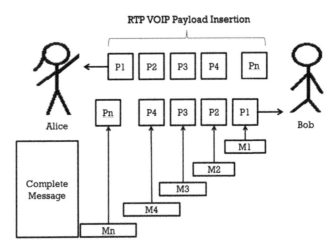

FIGURE 9.8 RTP Delayed Packet Modification

the hidden message content. The data hiding application then reinserts the packet back into the stream (after a few seconds of delay). Once the packet arrives at the destination (now significantly delayed), the receiving application discards the packet (it is never used), since it has already compensated for it earlier. However, a listening application recognizes the delayed packet and extracts it, and recovers the payload to rebuild the original message.

IP LAYER DATA HIDING, THE TTL FIELD

Since virtually any protocol at any layer is susceptible to data hiding, we decided to examine the work horse of Internet routing the IP packet. The Internet Protocol Layer IPv4 as shown in Figure 9.9 still constitutes the bulk of both UDP and TCP delivery.

Examining the layout of the protocol fields that make up the IP Header, we see for standard packets there are 20 bytes of data defined without optional values. The fields all have very specific purposes, for example, assigning the source and destination addresses, defining the type of service, checksum, or underlying protocol. One interesting field is the 8 bit or 1 byte time to live or TTL field. Due to the fact that IP is a "best effort" protocol, meaning exactly that, it will do its best to deliver the packet to the ultimate destination. Thus forced the creation of a mechanism that would end the life of a packet if it simply could not be delivered to the destination. Packet travels from router to router in search of a path to the ultimate destination. Each time this occurs the TTL field is decremented by one, once the TTL is decremented to zero the packet is discarded. This prevents packets that cannot be delivered from looping forever and clogging the network.

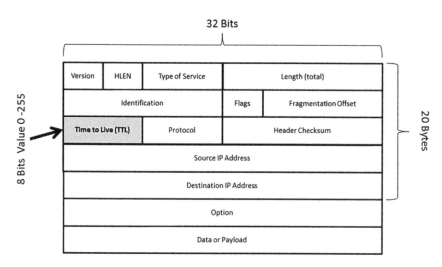

FIGURE 9.9 Internet Protocol Stack

Due to the intelligent nature of the modern routing networks we have today most packets arrive at their destination in just a few hops. There does not seem to be definitive statistics on average routes a typical IP packet takes. Domestic traffic I have witnessed passes typically through 8–15 routes, far less than the 255 that TTL allows for. Therefore, we rarely, if ever, exhaust the TTL before arriving at the destination, unless the destination is unreachable. Therefore, we could allocate the upper 2 bits of the TTL for data hiding without effecting packet delivery. In Figure 9.10, we have defined what each packet would look like. The default would be hex 3F for all packets (or 63 routes possible), leaving the upper 2 bits available for data embedding with every packet.

In Figure 9.11 we provide an example of how this would function. If we would like to stego into the IP stream the word "H I D E." First we convert the

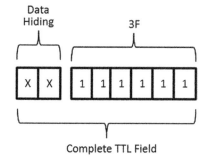

FIGURE 9.10 TTL Field Break-Down for Data Hiding

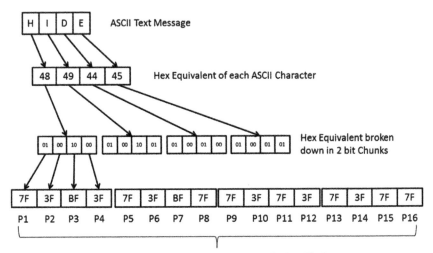

Sequence of IP Packet TTL Values to Convey the "HIDE" Message

FIGURE 9.11 Details of the TTL Data Hiding Scheme

characters into ASCII hex values. For example a capital H = 48 Hex. We then further break down these values into four 2 bit nibbles. In turn each of those 2 bit nibbles becomes the two upper bits of the TTL value, with the lower 6 bits always equal to the standard 3F or x x 1 1 1 1 1 1. The x x value is replaced by the 2 bit nibbles. By inserting these nibbles into the TTL values and forming a sequence of 16 IP packets, we can successfully transfer the message H I D E. It may seem incomprehensible to send a 1 MB file using this method as that would take ~4 million packets, since we can only send ¼ of each byte in each packet. However, when you consider the number of packets that would be necessary to stream music or video for an hour say, how many IP packets would that be?

INVESTIGATING PROTOCOL DATA HIDING

From an investigative perspective analyzing the protocol requires a network protocol analyzer or sniffer. Wireshark is a great tool for examining the details of such protocols. Once you suspect this type of behavior is occurring you can utilize Wireshark to capture the RTP packets flowing between two entities. At that point, detailed analysis of the headers of the payload section of each RTP packet is performed to detect inserted values. This may sound completely impossible or impractical. Actually, since Wireshark has powerful search and filtering capabilities, and the headers of the packets are quite regular, detecting the rogue packets is possible with some effort.

When attempting to detect the delayed packet hiding method, you are specifically looking for packet sequence numbers that are delayed. Sorting by the packet timestamps and writing a simple python script that will identify packets delayed more than a couple seconds is possible. Those of you that are more affluent with SNORT or other intrusion detection sensors, can come up with other rules and triggers that could constantly monitor for such aberrant behaviors.

SUMMARY

As you can see with patience, ingenuity and care embedding hidden information with Internet protocols is quite reasonable. With so many billions of messages, Web requests, VoIP, streaming music, and video that generate a quadrillion packets a day on the Internet we could easily find a way to hide small or even large amounts of information. This coupled with Zombies, Trojans, Keyloggers, and other malicious code left behind by worms and viruses, the question is how much information is leaking from your organization right now?

References

Rowland, C. (1997). Covert channels in the TCP/IP protocol suite. *First Monday, 2*(5). <http://firstmonday.org/htbin/cgiwrap/bin/ojs/inde9.php/fm/article/view/528/449>

SNORT (2012). Open source network intrusion prevention and detection system (IDS/IPS). <http://www.snort.org>.

WIRESHARK (2012). Network protocol analyzer information. <http://www.wireshark.org/>.

This page is intentionally left blank

## CHAPTER 10

Forensics and Anti-Forensics

INFORMATION IN THIS CHAPTER:

- Introduction
- Anti-Forensics—Hiding your tracks
- Forensics

INTRODUCTION

It has long been rumored that al-Qaeda uses data hiding techniques to covertly exchange documents related to terrorist plots. Over the last 10 years, al-Qaeda manuals have been found to contain techniques for covert communications using steganography programs and techniques. On May 16th, 2011, an Austrian named Maqsood Lodin was questioned by police in Berlin, Germany. Hidden in his underpants were a digital storage device and memory cards. The memory card contained files including a video. After thorough analysis, German investigators determined that over 100 files had been hidden in the video using steganographic techniques and protected with a password. Upon cracking the password, the files were determined to include terrorist training manuals and future plots to seize cruise ships and attacks on Europe.[1]

In today's digital world, data hiding has reinvented itself for use in digital covert communications with one common goal—avoiding detection. And knowing the anti-forensic techniques for avoiding detection ensures that weak data hiding techniques are avoided. This knowledge provides the basis for refining a methodology for using data hiding with greater confidence in the most critical of situations. This chapter is intended to provide additional Forensic and Anti-Forensic techniques for data hiding not covered in the preceding chapters, but will not include techniques for hiding digital storage devices and memory cards in underpants.

---

[1] Documents reveal al-Qaeda's plans for seizing cruise ships, carnage in Europe—http://edition.cnn.com/2012/04/30/world/al-qaeda-documents-future/.

193

ANTI-FORENSICS—HIDING YOUR TRACKS

One of the most common oversights of data hiding that users make is that they leave the remains of not only the carrier file with the hidden message, but also the original carrier file. As demonstrated in previous chapters, there are many techniques for identifying the differences between two identical-*looking* files. As a result, it's highly recommended that the original virgin carrier file be deleted after creating the carrier file with the payload. This is assuming that the original isn't converted into the carrier file with the payload, hence removing the existence of the original virgin carrier file.

Evidence of the data hiding program should also be removed from the host computer. If a steganography program is found on a suspect computer, most likely there are carrier files on the computer as well. If these carrier files are found, then the only thing between the investigator and revealing the hidden message is typically the password used in the data hiding program used to hide the data. If this password is used in other programs such as the login password, the investigator is that much closer to cracking the key to the hidden data. Optionally, some users delete the data hiding program following its use. And don't forget about Recycle Bin or slack space.

When attempting to hide files in digital photographs it's recommended that you choose a custom-made digital photograph rather than one that is common-place. For example, don't use a file from Google Images. A common file such as this might allow an investigator to obtain the original file from somewhere else other than the suspect computer, thereby allowing the investigator to compare the original file and the suspect file to identify differences as a result of hidden content in the suspect file. For example, there are hash databases maintained by agencies and vendors. Hashing the suspect picture and comparing it to the known hash will immediately validate the suspicions when the hash computes differently.

Storing the data hiding program and carrier files on removable storage is a great first step towards eliminating evidence, but that's assuming that the rest of the equipment, if not yourself, are not part of an investigation. Let's continue by reviewing additional anti-forensic data hiding best practices.

Data Hiding Passwords

Passwords are equally important to consider. As always, remember to use strong passwords when hiding a message within a carrier file. Common recommendations include:

- Use a password different from the operating system password, stored passwords in the browser, or passwords used for network services.
- Use a combination of upper/lower alphanumeric characters and special characters.

- If you must store the password somewhere, consider using Bruce Schneier's PasswordSafe http://passwordsafe.sourceforge.net/.

Many of the data hiding programs require a user-defined password. When hiding contents using a password it's commonly recommended that strong passwords be used. But there are strong passwords, and then **strong** passwords. During my teaching days, I was amazed with the number of administrators unaware of the hidden characters on a keyboard that can be used to create a **strong** password. Most dictionary and brute force attack mechanisms don't even incorporate these characters. It's also a fantastic way to make hell of a determined cracker's efforts.

Examples:

- [CTRL]+[ALT]+[C] gives ©
- [CTRL]+[ALT]+[R] gives ®
- [CTRL]+[ALT]+[T] gives ™
- [CTRL]+[ALT]+[E] gives €

Figure 10.1 provides a more comprehensive list of special characters for Windows.

Using one or more special characters in your password will allow you to avoid many types of brute force password cracking programs. This is preferred technique for not only data hiding password protection, but computer security in general. In addition, simply increasing the quantity of characters used for the password can exponentially increase the effort required to crack the password. These techniques will prevent the investigator from using your password to view your hidden data.

Hiding Your Tracks

In Windows, you can use the cleanmgr utility to wipe your system clean of any remaining evidence of data hiding software. It is not a silver bullet, but a quick way to cleanse a machine. From the command line, simply run:

```
c:\cleanmgr²
```

This will prompt the user to pick a drive to cleanse. The command will clean the following:

- Temporary Internet Files.
- Temporary Setup Files.
- Temporary Offline Files.
- Downloaded Program Files.

---

² Cleanmgr.exe—http://support.microsoft.com/kb/253597.

- Empty the Recycle Bin.
- Windows Temporary Files.
- Optional Windows Components Not Being Used.
- Old chkdsk Files.
- Catalog Files for the Content Indexer.

Windows also keeps track of every program that you run and places the most frequently run programs in the Start Panel. To clear this list of programs in Windows 7 right-click on Start and Click Properties. Then deselect the check-boxes under Privacy, as shown in Figure 10.2. These include "Store and display recently opened programs in the Start menu" and "Store and display recently opened items in the Start menu and taskbar."

You can also click "Customize" in the Start Menu and set "Number of recent programs to display" and "Number of recent items to display in Jump lists" to zeroes as shown in Figure 10.3.

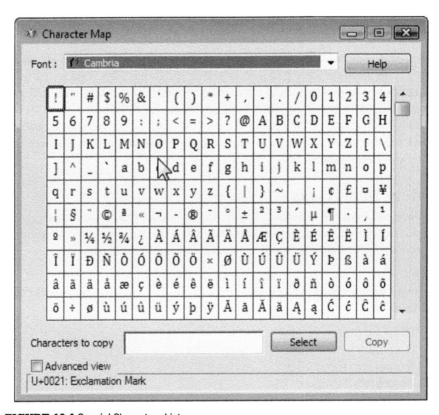

FIGURE 10.1 Special Characters List

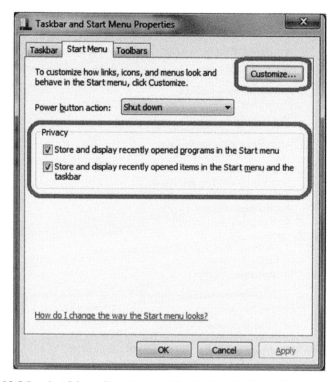

FIGURE 10.2 Deselect Privacy Checkboxes to Disable Recently Opened Items

These settings will also allow you to eliminate "last run program" evidence.

FORENSICS

There are a variety of ways to detect if a suspect system contains data hiding software. These options may include:

- Data hiding software applications still exist on the suspect computer.
- Cached website pages indicate the suspect accessed web pages that provide data hiding software.
- Cached images indicate the suspect accessed and potentially downloaded data hiding software.
- Remaining artifacts indicated that data hiding software was once installed or used on the system.

  - Registry.
  - Remaining files left after the uninstall.
  - "Thumb" files.

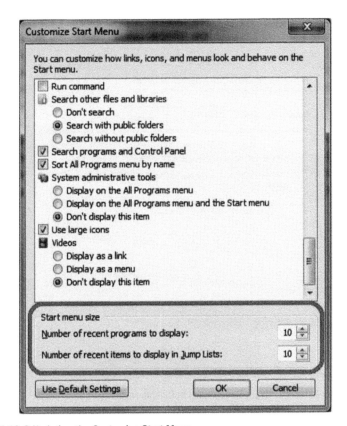

FIGURE 10.3 Updating the Customize Start Menu

Looking for Data Hiding Software

It may seem obvious to most people that a quick review of a system may instantly reveal the evidence of data hiding software on the suspect computer. Everything from viewing the installed programs to searching directories may reveal installed packages.

For example, in Ubuntu Linux you can obtain a list of installed packages by running:

```
# sudo dpkg --get-selections > listofpkgs
```

It's important to note that some data hiding programs don't require any installation whatsoever, and as a result can be run from a CD, floppy, thumb drive, etc. To view the Most Recently Used (MRU) programs in Windows, simply run regedit and view the following key:

```
User Key: [HKEY_CURRENT_USER\Software\Microsoft\Windows\CurrentVersion\
    Explorer\RunMRU]
```

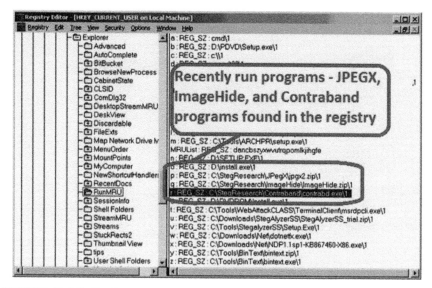

FIGURE 10.4 Finding Steganography Programs in the Registry

Figure 10.4 shows the list of Most Recently Used programs in the Windows Registry. In this example, when we review the registry we can see a number of steganography programs listed including: Contraband, ImageHide, and JPEGX.

There are a variety of other ways to review these remaining artifacts left behind by previously installed data hiding software. A number of tools exist that automate this type of analysis. Let's take a look at some of the most common programs.

Finding Remaining Artifacts

It is common for experienced users to delete the data hiding program after use, or to run it from removable media. Both may leave trace evidence that can be extremely useful during an investigation. Everything from registry artifacts to temporary directories may provide an alternative avenue to the investigator when investigating a suspect computer.

But there is an alternative way to identify that a system contains (or used to contain) steganography software. Various organizations such as the Department of Defense (DoD) and National Institute of Standards and Technology (NIST) have created file hashes for common *.dll's and other files created during the installation of the data hiding software. Software packages now exist that allow an investigator to scan a machine for these files and compare the hashes to determine if a data hiding program was once installed. These programs can sometimes also look for artifacts left behind in the registry, even after the data hiding program has been removed.

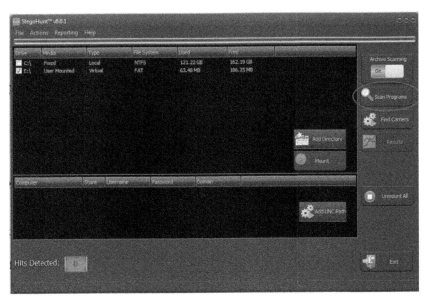

FIGURE 10.5 StegoHunt Scan Program Selection

WetStone Technologies StegoHunt™

WetStone's StegoHunt Software provides investigators with the ability to search for both known Steganography / Data Hiding programs and will also identify carrier files (images, audio, video, and documents) that contain hidden information. WetStone has collected known steganography and data hiding programs for over a decade and their repository contains over 2000 known data hiding applications. StegoHunt™[3] uses a combination of a proprietary Fibonacci and standard MD5 or SHA hash signatures to accurately identify these known applications used to conceal data. The program can scan Drives, Directories, Forensic Image files, and networked computers for the existence of such threats (see Figure 10.5).

Once the scan completes, StegoHunt provides detailed results either in printable reports or a results grid shown in Figure 10.6. The results grid provides information regarding each file detected and correlates that file with the known Steganography or Data Hiding program that it is associated with. StegoHunt also preserves the Modified, Accessed, and Created times, the Forensic Hash of the file, the filename, directory, and the original file name that was used by the application. (Note: in some cases suspects change the filename and file extension associated with nefarious programs to conceal their activities.)

---

[3] StegoHunt™—http://www.wetstonetech.com.

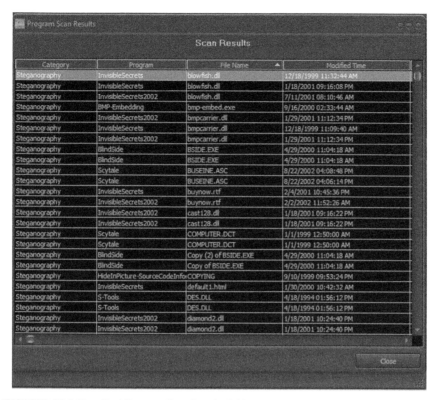

FIGURE 10.6 StegoHunt Program Scan Results Grid

Also, included with StegoHunt is the ability to scan for carrier files (the files that actually contain the hidden data). This function invokes a search for images, audio, video, and document files that may contain hidden information. The algorithms that perform this examination are quite sophisticated and can detect slight anomalies within images and multimedia carriers that are created when embedding hidden information. In addition, the function detects signature and structural artifacts that often occur from data hiding activities. Examining the results of the Carrier scan provides a summary of findings that pinpoints files that are suspected of containing hidden data. In addition, each detected file contains a category and detect-code that provides further information regarding the details of the findings (see Figure 10.7).

Once suspected carrier files have been detected, StegoHunt's StegoAnalyst and StegoBreak modules perform deep inspection and perform cracking operations against the suspect carriers to recover the hidden data.

StegoAnalyst provides detailed visual and auditory inspection of image, audio, video, and document files with a plethora of tools to render these carriers that highlight data hiding activities (see Figure 10.8).

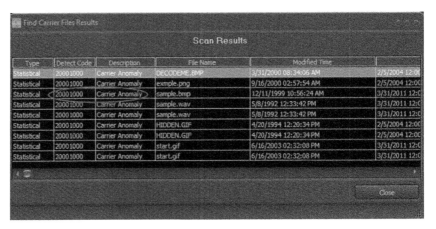

FIGURE 10.7 StegoHunt Carrier Scan Results Grid

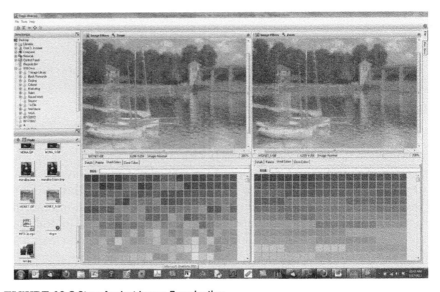

FIGURE 10.8 StegoAnalyst Image Examination

StegoBreak performs dictionary and/or brute force attacks against suspected carrier files. If successful, the attacks will return the passphrases used by the identified steganography applications. Extraction is then done by using the known steganography or data hiding threat with the suspect file and the discovered passphrase in order to extract the hidden payload (see Figure 10.9).

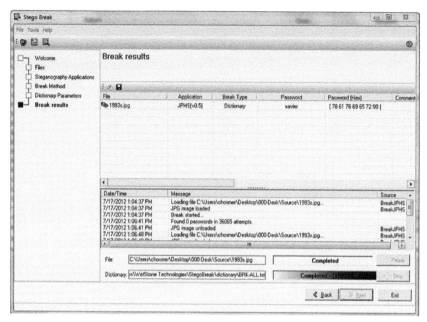

FIGURE 10.9 StegoBreak Cracking Automation

Identifying and View Cached Images (Cache Auditing Tools)

In addition to scanning for data hiding software itself, an investigator can attempt to identify websites commonly known for providing data hiding software. A suspect computer may warrant an analysis of visited sites and surfing habits. It's quite possible that the data hiding software was locally downloaded using the same computer. Analyzing the visited URLs and cached images can be a great way to determine whether a suspect computer warrants a full investigation. It is also important to determine if the suspect was a member of any online chat groups to determine posts that may be relevant to the investigation.

To a forensic investigator it would seem important to review not only static images on the suspect computer, but also cached images. If a suspect deletes the data hiding program and carrier and payload files, the cached directories may still house relevant images. This could provide additional proof of access to data hiding software sites. In the case of a terrorist, cached images may reveal images that were uploaded to a terrorist site for download by another terrorist in the cell. Analysis of this cached image may reveal use of data hiding and therefore hidden messages.

STG Cache Audit

STG Cache Audit (www.snapfiles.com/screenshots/stgcache.htm) is an advanced cache, cookie, and history viewer that runs on Windows and that allows you to

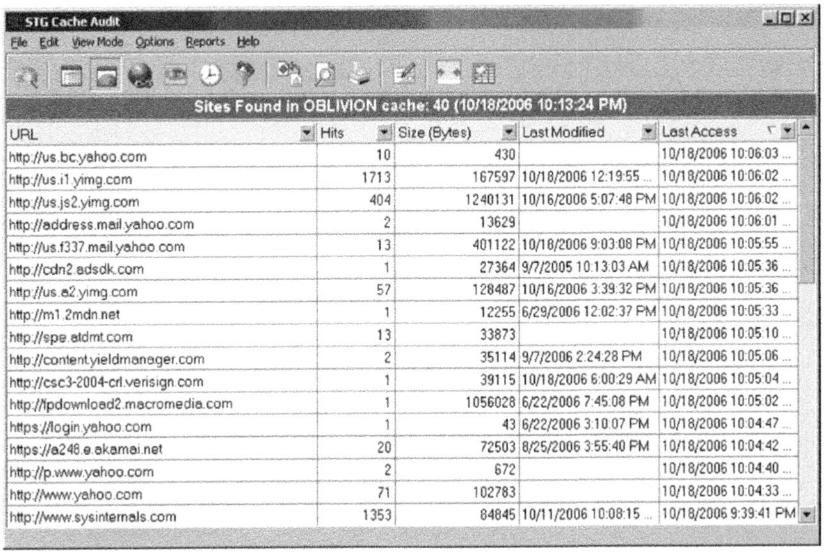

FIGURE 10.10 STG Cache Audit Site View

investigate web surfing habits of a suspect machine. You can set filter words and instantly view sites that relate to certain keywords, sort the results by different criteria, and create a detailed report. The "Site View" allows one to see which sites were visited how often. Figure 10.10 shows the results of running STG Cache Audit on suspect machine to quickly identify sites visited by the suspect.

The "History View" allows the user to chronologically list the surfing events as they occurred. The investigator can also drill down into a specific URL as shown in Figure 10.11.

The user can also export the results to many formats including HTML, text, CSV, and an Excel spreadsheet. This is a nice piece of evidentiary information to the overall investigation.

Evidence in Thumbnails

Thumbnails are another type of cached information that can be analyzed on a suspect computer. Thumbnails are found in Windows Operating Systems and are intended to allow a quick view of files residing in a folder. Unbeknownst to most people, this view also simultaneously creates an associated thumbs.db file in the same folder that stores a miniature version of the images. Thumbs. db files also store the first page of things such as a PowerPoint presentation.

Although this information may not identify the data hiding directly, it does allow an investigator to identify suspicious data that was once hidden within

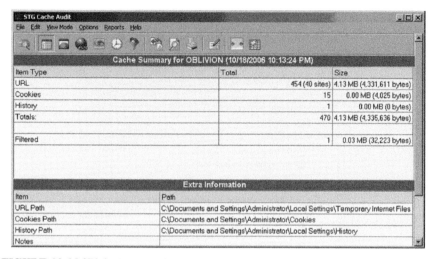

FIGURE 10.11 STG Cache Audit History View

another file. For example, if a terrorist has a diagram for a building and then hides that diagram in a carrier file using steganography, a cached version of that original diagram remains in the thumbs.db file. If the terrorist is wise enough to remove the steganography program, the diagram, and the carrier file, they may not have covered all of their tracks, because a copy of it still resides in the thumbs.db file!

To view the thumbnails database, one must first go into Folder Options, select View, and deselect "Hide protected operating system files" as shown in Figure 10.12. (In Windows 7, within Windows Explorer, go to Organize and then Folder and Search Options).

Windows Explorer will then display thumbs.db in the current folder as shown in Figure 10.13. Note that it's always there, just not visible unless you unhide it.

Thumbnails of images are stored automatically in the current folder's thumbs.db file unless the user has explicitly disabled them. This goes for Windows ME, Windows 2000, Windows XP, and Windows 2003. One notable is that for Windows 2000, the thumbs.db is actually stored in an ADS (Alternate Data Stream), as long as it's on an NTFS partition, and therefore will not appear in the folder at all.

Starting with Windows Vista and Windows 7, the thumbs.db files are stored in central location for each user in %userprofile%\AppData\Local\Microsoft\Windows\Explorer (see Figure 10.14).

There are a number of freeware and commercial tools for viewing and analyzing thumbs.db files. Thumbnail Database Viewer available at: http://www.itsamples.com/thumbnail-database-viewer.html is a freeware utility for viewing the

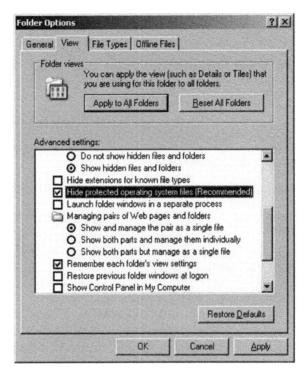

FIGURE 10.12 Displaying a thumbs.db File in Windows

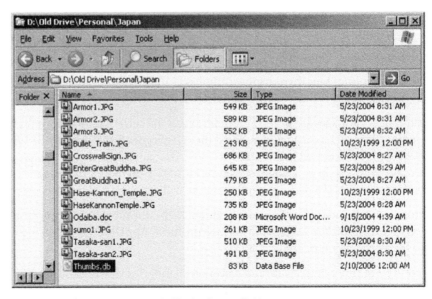

FIGURE 10.13 Thumbs.db Revealed in the Current Folder

Name	Date modified	Type	Size
ExplorerStartupLog.etl	1/25/2011 1:39 PM	ETL File	40 KB
ExplorerStartupLog_RunOnce.etl	9/23/2011 9:13 AM	ETL File	16 KB
thumbcache_32	9/2/2011 1:06 PM	Data Base File	1,024 KB
thumbcache_96	9/24/2011 11:07 PM	Data Base File	10,240 KB
thumbcache_256	9/2/2011 1:06 PM	Data Base File	6,144 KB
thumbcache_1024	9/2/2011 1:06 PM	Data Base File	7,168 KB
thumbcache_idx	9/19/2011 11:37 AM	Data Base File	26 KB
thumbcache_sr	9/2/2011 1:06 PM	Data Base File	1 KB

FIGURE 10.14 Windows Vista and Windows 7 Centrally Stored Thumbs.db Files

database. Within the tool choose the thumbs.db you want to analyze, or use the search function to find all of them. The viewer will allow you to view current and previous thumbnails and build an audit trail of pictures, videos, powerpoint presentations, etc. that once resided on the system (see Figure 10.15).

Another interesting fact about thumbnails is that they are stored in the thumbs. db file even after the graphic file has been deleted! They will remain there forever, unless manually deleted. If a suspect is suspected of terrorism and deletes all of the images, a miniature version of them still resides in the thumbs.db.

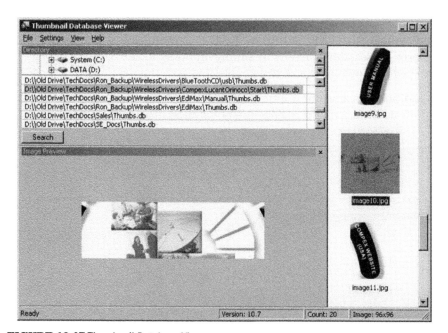

FIGURE 10.15 Thumbnail Database Viewer

If the filesystem is encrypted using EFS, unpatched Microsoft systems will still display the miniature versions of the images in the thumbs.db unencrypted!

It may also be possible that the suspect moved these images to removable media. Copying these from a hard disk drive to a USB thumb drive still leaves behind the thumbs.db on the original hard drive, thereby leaving critical evidence on the main suspect computer even if the removable media is nowhere to be found. This is by far one of the most effective ways to determine what images were once stored on a suspect computer and can be the single best way to crack a case.

Users can disable the use of a thumbs.db. For example, in Windows 7 a user can cover their tracks by copying the registry entry shown in Figure 10.16 to a notepad file and saving it as disablethumbsdb.reg.

Now simply double-click on the file to add it to the registry, and then reboot. Please edit the windows registry at your own risk.

Searching for Hidden Directories and Files

In a previous chapter we covered Alternate Data Streams (ADS) in Windows. There are a handful of other tools that do allow one to identify files hidden in Alternate Data Streams. Let's take a look at LNS.

LNS

LNS (www.ntsecurity.nu/toolbox/lns/) is a freeware tool for Windows used for identifying hidden files in Alternate Data Streams on a suspect computer. It can perform the search recursively by simply inputting the directory or drive to be searched as shown in Figure 10.17.

In addition, streams.exe is a program available from Microsoft's sysinternals website at, http://technet.microsoft.com/en-us/sysinternals/bb897440.

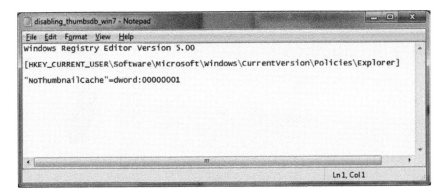

FIGURE 10.16 Using the Registry to Disable Thumbs.db Files in Windows 7

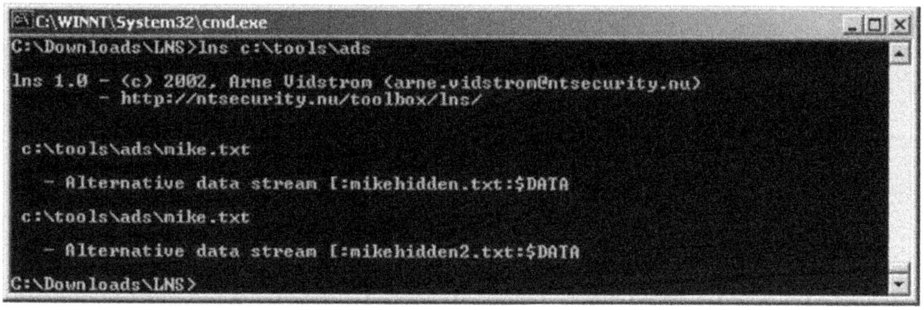

FIGURE 10.17 LNS Alternate Data Streams Scanner

Network IDS

With the prevalence of network intrusion detection and prevention systems in most corporate environments, corporations are looking to track not only incoming threats, but outgoing threats such as corporate espionage, objectionable content, and exposure of confidential information.

The foundation for creating signatures to detect data hiding involves building rules that include each individual signature for every data hiding program. In addition, these signatures can vary from version to version. Therefore it's important to distinguish these not only in the signatures, but the resulting report output including the program identified and the program version. Other relevant information would include the source and destinations IPs so as to assist the investigator with identifying the suspect machine.

A sniffer can be very effective for testing your rules and ensuring proper mappings. Using wireshark we can sniff the wire during the transmission of a carrier file or covert transmission Figure 10.18. demonstrates a capture that reveals the Hiderman signature identified by "CDN." Although it's possible this could be a random sequence of characters, the probability is low, and therefore it's a strong possibility that this is the signature of our Hiderman program.

We can therefore build a Snort signature to detect this. A lazy man's version of Snort is provided on Backtrack http://www.backtrack-linux.org[4] comes with a full install of Snort. Once you have Snort installed, you can begin to add your data hiding IDS rules. IDS rules typically generate a plethora of false positives, so it's important to ensure accuracy of your rules (the longer the signature string, the greater the accuracy). Rules can include content matches in ASCII or Hexadecimal. Because steganography signatures don't always include ASCII mappings, hexadecimal notations are typically more effective. The following demonstrates both options:

Signature syntax for an ASCII notation:

```
Alert tcp any any <> any any (msg:"Message"; content:"content";)
```

---

[4] BackTrack http://www.backtrack-linux.org/.

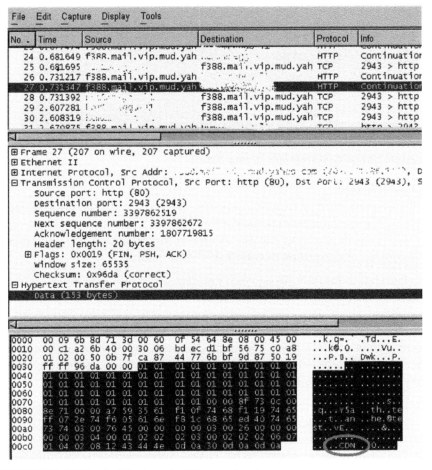

FIGURE 10.18 Wireshark Capture of a Hiderman Signature

Signature syntax for hexadecimal notation:

```
Alert tcp any any <> any any (msg:"Message"; content:"|hex string|";)
```

The following example demonstrates the signatures for Hiderman in both ASCII and hexadecimal notation. Note the signature located in the content section of the rule.

```
Alert tcp any any <> any any (msg:"Hiderman Detected"; content:"CDN";)
Alert tcp any any <> any any (msg:"Hiderman Detected"; content:"43 44
    4E";)
```

The previous example would probably have a large number of false positives due to the simplicity of the signature, but the next example demonstrates a longer signature string for the Jpegx steganography program. The signature for Jpegx V2.1.1 is "36 45 35 3B 32 00 00." This type of signature is difficult to represent in ASCII form, so the only way to identify it is by its hexadecimal notation. Building a rule for Jpegx V2.1.1 would yield:

```
Alert tcp any any <> any any (msg:"Jpegx V2.1.1 Detected"; content:"36
    45 35 3B 32 00 00";)
```

If you have a fairly complex string, hexadecimal notation may provide better accuracy than ASCII strings anyways, so sticking with hexadecimal is the best way to go.

If we can detect steganography over the wire, we now have the ability to identify potentially malicious people on our network. In addition, we have the ability to identify incoming carrier files from the Internet to an internal suspect. Commercial vendors have yet to create IDS signatures for detecting steganography. Most Intrusion Detection Systems (IDS) and Data Leakage Prevention Systems (DLP) vendors do not have signatures for detecting steganography over the network. Perhaps we'll see this area mature over the coming years and emerge as a new option for detecting steganography.

SUMMARY

As demonstrated in this chapter, a suspect has a very challenging task of cleansing a system. With the arsenal available to an investigator, a determined investigator has a respectable chance of finding one or more data hiding programs installed or once installed on a machine. Additionally, cached files, thumbnails, and other evidence may reside on the suspect computer. If the suspect is to have any chance he must stick with removable media and properly cover his tracks. Otherwise the only other reasonable way is to destroy the media or disk is through low-level sanitization. The techniques in this chapter provide insight into forensic and anti-forensic techniques when dealing with data hiding.

References

BackTrack http://www.backtrack-linux.org/.

cleanmgr.exe. <http://support.microsoft.com/kb/253597>.

Documents reveal al-Qaeda's plans for seizing cruise ships, carnage in Europe. <http://edition.cnn.com/2012/04/30/world/al-qaeda-documents-future/>.

StegoHunt™. <http://www.wetstonetech.com>.

This page is intentionally left blank

Mitigation Strategies

INFORMATION IN THIS CHAPTER:

- Forensic Investigation
- Mitigation

FORENSIC INVESTIGATION

We have all heard the statement "It is like trying to find a needle in a haystack." For historical purposes, the original saying is typically credited to St. Thomas More in 1532 when he wrote "to seek out one line in his books would be to go looking for a needle in a meadow." As difficult as that sounds, a number of years ago during a presentation at George Mason University, I compared discovering steganography to finding that proverbial needle in a haystack. However, I was immediately corrected by Dr. Neil Johnson who was in the audience that day. Neil stated that a more accurate description would be "trying to find a piece of straw in a haystack."

We have certainly made progress in uncovering data hiding and steganography activities during the last decade through the process of data collection, direct experimentation, and deep analysis of "known steganography" programs. Although each investigation and circumstances are different, the following chart provides a basic model for identifying steganography and discovering the hidden messages that lie beneath (see Figure 11.1).

Step 1 Steganography Use Discovery

Step 1 requires access to the suspect data storage containers. We must create a forensically sound image (or perform a write blocking scan) of the suspect's data storage devices. This would include local storage devices, remote storage, memory sticks, SD Cards, etc. Once obtained, a scan would be performed to identify known steganography or data hiding programs. During this step we

213

Data Hiding. http://dx.doi.org/10.1016/B978-1-59-749743-5.00011-0

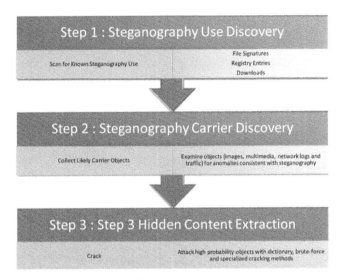

FIGURE 11.1 General Steganography Forensic Discovery

are looking not only for executable files, but also collateral files, and registry entries related to these known steganography programs. During this stage, we would also examine any Web history, downloaded applications, and network searches performed by the suspect that would point to an interest in steganography. This step is quite important in order to potentially streamline the process in Steps 2 and 3. The more we know about the specific steganography programs utilized by the suspect, the more targeted the subsequent steps would be. For example, if we found evidence that the suspect had downloaded JP Hide and Seek, (abbreviated as JPHS), and the program was found on his or her computer and was last accessed three days ago, the subsequent steps would be more critical. Furthermore, if this is the only steganography program we found evidence of, we could deduce the following:

a. JPHS can only perform steganography on jpeg files (thus we narrow the field of possible carriers).

b. Last access time changes on jpeg files in the last three days would be possible cover files.

c. Last modified time changes on jpeg files in the last three days may contain possible steganographic embedding.

Note: US State and Local Law Enforcement can obtain a free tool from the Electronic Crime Technology Center of Excellence (ECTCOE) called Trait Analytic Program Search or T.A.P.S. that will perform Step 1 (NIJ).[1]

---

[1] NIJ, Electronic Crime Technology Center of Excellence—http://www.ectcoe.net/resources/tools.

Step 2 Steganography Carrier Discovery

Based on the results from Step 1, we would collect likely carrier files. This could be filtered by type of carrier, time and date, or other case-relevant data. Once the possible carrier files have been collected we typically apply three types of analysis to each of the collected objects:

a. We first run signature-based anomaly detection algorithms against the suspect carrier files. Many steganography programs modify characteristics of the carrier file in ways that are detectable. A simple example would be the steganography program Camouflage, which appends data after the end of file marker. Signature detection algorithms will easily pickup and report this anomaly and identify the offending files.

b. Next, we run more sophisticated blind steganography detection algorithms. These methods calculate statistics on each object in question and compare those statistics against "known good" models of images and multimedia files. Any outliers are reported and further analysis would be recommended.

c. Finally, a human analyst examines the results from Steps 1 and 2, and then examines the objects manually. In this step visual, auditory and multifactor rendering is applied to the suspect files. For example, if we suspect that LSB embedding was performed on a True Color image (BMP, PNG, etc.) we would render only the LSB values and determine visually if the distribution of values in the LSB follows the image, or if the data is random indicating a steganographic replacement of the LSB values.

Step 3 Hidden Content Extraction

Once we have narrowed the field on confirmed to a high degree of certainty, we have digital objects that contain hidden information we can proceed to the cracking step. Unlike encryption where standardization does exist for encrypted files and these encrypted files are interoperable, this is not the case with Steganography. Each steganography program performs hiding using differing methods. Thus knowledge of the Steganography program is an almost essential ingredient for cracking. The most common ways of discovering the steganography program that was used by the suspect are as follows:

a. Program was discovered during Step 1—Steganography Use Discovery.
b. Program was deduce based upon the characteristics found during Step 2— Steganography Carrier Discovery.

Once we established the likely program(s), we attack the carrier file with either known passwords (dictionaries, extracted suspect information) or by using brute force password generation. Once these are generated we can apply each potential password using the likely identified program or develop software that will mimic the behavior of the program in an automated fashion. Finally, certain carrier files content can be directly cracked (without password guessing) due to weaknesses in their construction or flaws in their key management methods.

MITIGATION

Defining a mitigation strategy requires a thorough understanding of what it is you're trying to protect against. In 1995, Dan Farmer and Wieste Venema released their network vulnerability scanning tool SATAN (Security Administrator Tool for Analyzing Networks). This was one of the original network vulnerability scanning tools. Dan Farmer's thought process was how better to protect your network than by trying to hack into it and use that information to determine how to better fortify your network. This brought on a new era of network security focused on penetration testing and ethical hacking.

This approach can also be applied to data hiding and your network to determine the effectiveness of your defense-in-depth strategy. By exercising some of the tools and techniques outlined in this book, you can determine how well your layers of security identify evidence and behaviors of data hiding techniques.

Data hiding activities can lead to corporate espionage, covert communications, child exploitation, data breaches, and other malicious activities. For example, when companies are concerned about personal identifiable information (PII) breaches, they commonly implement a DLP (Data Leakage Prevention) product and define rules around data that resembles their PII data. But when that data is hidden using a sophisticated technique, it becomes much more difficult to detect.

How people hide data varies greatly. The examples in this book only scratch the surface in terms of the broadness of techniques. But in most cases the approach and behavior of data hiding follows general methodology. Most commonly, a user downloads a data hiding application from the Internet, and uses this to hide their payload or content within a carrier file. Then posts that file on the Web for the recipient to download, or communicates it over the network via E-mail, ftp, or other means. Let's take a closer look at this process step by step (see Figure 11.2.).

1. *Download Program*—The most common method of data hiding involves a user downloading a canned tool designed for hiding data. These programs are available for not only computers, but mobile devices as well.
2. *Install Program*—When the program is installed a few things occur. First the device identifies install behavior, and many times the installation will include multiple files. In the case of Windows, one or more dlls may be installed, the registry may be updated, and an executable is loaded.

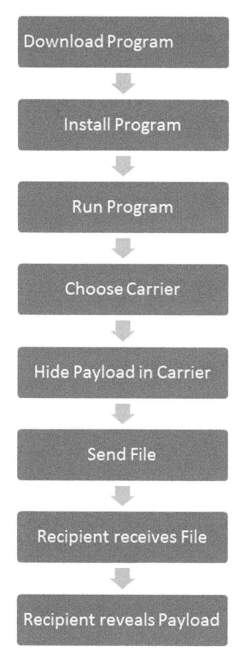

FIGURE 11.2 Data Hiding using a Program

3. *Run program*—When the program is used to hide the data, it may delete the original payload file after it has hidden it in the carrier file.
4. *Choose carrier*—The carrier file chosen for hiding data is typically dependent upon the data hiding program, and can range from a JPEG, to an MP3, or even a PDF. The format of the payload file may also hinge on the program used to hide in the carrier file. For example, a schematic may need to be changed to a format that the program understands, such as converting a Visio diagram to a PDF.
5. *Hide payload in carrier*—Largely dependent on the program, this step involves inserting the payload, and choosing numerous other options specific to the program. This may involve options for where and how the data is hidden, as well as possible encryptions options and a password. Once the file is saved, this carrier file is a hybrid of the original, except now it has content hidden within it. As a result, its makeup, layout, and even format may change (e.g. changing the file from a JPEG to a BMP).
6. *Send file*—Although the file could be carried out on a thumb drive, most commonly the carrier file is sent over the network. This can range from sending from a personal E-mail account to a recipient, posting it to a site for download, uploading it to an FTP server, or embedding it covertly in a network protocol. But in all of these circumstances there's one commonality—it's sent over the network. Therefore, it's possible that a variety of detection devices can be used to identify the carrier file, or anomalous behavior.
7. *Recipient receives file*—Again, this involves another network hop, and therefore another possibility for detection. Whether the user downloads it from a Website, retrieves it via E-mail, or pulls it down from an FTP server, it has still traversed the network.
8. *Recipient reveals payload*—The recipient will most likely need to use the same program as the sender for extracting the hidden content. This involves all of the previous steps outlined, thus providing another process for detection.

A more experienced user may use sophisticated techniques to hide data manually, rather than using a public tool. Since the manual approach is more of a one-off, it can make this more difficult to detect and mitigate, but the behaviors are very similar. Hiding the data via manual methods will most likely avoid the download and installation steps outlined in the life cycle diagram. But how data is hidden within the carrier file may be similar for manual methods and methods employing a software program or tool. Manual methods circumvent download and installation program detections. Many of these manual techniques have been detailed throughout the book.

So far we've outlined the steps involved with hiding data. But the burning question as this point is: how do detect this? This involves tools and techniques that analyze data-at-rest and data-in-transit.

Network Technologies for detecting Data Hiding

Companies are using their defense-in-depth strategy to identify and counter data hiding techniques. Statistics suggest that data is most frequently hidden using free data hiding tools available over the Internet. So while although covert VOIP or Wireless transmissions can occur, it is more common to come across a malicious user who has used a known data hiding application to commit crimes such as child exploitation or corporate espionage. Since this is more common, the potential for damage is higher due to how frequently this occurs when compared to a VOIP or Wireless attack (see Figure 11.3).

Today there are a variety of products for detecting evidence of data hiding techniques. For data-in-transit, there are network capture tools that allow for post-collection analysis of hidden data, for example in pcap files. Additionally, comprehensive monitoring products allow for correlation of multiple data points and presentation within a SIEM (Security Information Event Management) view. These products stem from Live network analysis tools such as IPS and MPS (malware protection systems). But finding hidden data is far more difficult than identifying a known malicious file. Additionally, hashes exist for common files such as common photos, but when an individual hides data within an unknown digital photo there is no hash to compare it to in order to determine if the original photo has been modified to hide data.

The following table details categories of products most likely in enterprise networks today that can be used as part of a defense-in-depth strategy for identifying, mitigating, and remediating data hiding activities. This includes

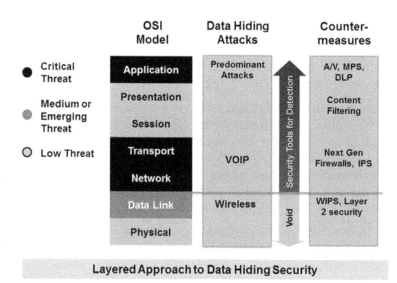

FIGURE 11.3 Layered Approach to Data Hiding Security

Table 11.1 Network Technologies for Detecting Data Hiding Activities

Technology	Detection, Mitigation, & Remediation capabilities
Intrusion Prevention System	Detect and block downloaded data hiding and steganography programs (App Blocking)
Malware Protection System	Sandbox, analyze, & block unknown executables & files
	Network Security Analytics & Forensics with add-on products
Anti-Virus	Quarantine & remove downloaded known data hiding and steganography programs
Next Generation Firewall (NGFW)	Application Signatures
	Application Protocol Decoding
	Network Heuristics (Behavioral)
Data Leakage Prevention (DLP)	Identify & block documents with company specific metadata
	Identify strings of data hidden within files (SS#, Credit Card, PII, PHI, etc.)
Wireless Intrusion Prevention System	Detect wireless protocol manipulation and block malicious extrusions
Content Filter	Detect and block data hiding program downloads
Jamming	Sanitization and re-encoding of files
Application Blocking	White Listing
	Black Listing
	Hash verification for known safe programs

data-in-transit traversing the network such as a file, as well as data hidden within network transmissions and protocols (see Table 1).

Most Intrusion Prevention Systems (IPS) are not fine tuned for detecting data hiding techniques and steganography programs. IPSs are best fit to detect the downloading of data hiding and steganography programs, or step 1 of our life-cycle wheel. Currently, most IPS products do not have the signatures for detecting the majority of these types of programs, but they could be. Many of the common programs have been profiled, and with minimal effort signatures could be created to detect this download activity.

Malware Protection Systems are designed to analyze unknown executables with malicious intent. By dumping an unknown executable into a virtual sandbox, the MPS analyzes the behavior of the executable when at runtime. Any installed or modified dlls, registry changes, services installed, and many other behaviors are identified and analyzed for unauthorized or anomalous activities synonymous with malcode. This heuristic (behavioral) analysis is a nice fit for identifying new data hiding or steganography programs that have not been profiled to date.

Anti-Virus seems like an obvious choice for detecting data hiding and steganography activities. In terms of programs, most are downloaded via the Internet, rather than sent over E-mail, so in this case A/V is not a good fit. But when people send E-mails with attachments with embedded hidden data created by these known programs, anti-virus could be a good solution for detecting and mitigating this activity. The shortcoming of A/V today is that most do not include a comprehensive set of signatures for detecting attachments with embedded hidden data.

Next Generation Firewalls (NGFW) provide a plethora of features that dwarf old school firewalls. The Application Protocol Decoding feature of these firewalls allows it to detect an embedded protocol within a protocol and various tunneling techniques. For some of the data hiding protocols, Application Protocol Decoding could provide a possible solution to some of these techniques, but further development in this area would be required. Additionally, Next Generation Firewalls also include heuristic analysis to analyze evasive techniques including protocols using proprietary encryption and other evasive techniques and misuse. Although Next Generation Firewalls lack out of the box data hiding and steganographic transmission detection, the policies contained within these products can be refined to detect some of these communications.

Data Leakage Prevention (DLP) can be used to detect files and documents with metadata. Policies can be created to track extrusions such as undesired metadata that should not leave the network. DLPs in general required a fair amount of tuning to detect metadata specific to the company or institution. But is important to note that data hiding programs that use obfuscation techniques or masking of data (e.g. encryption) will most likely not be detected by most DLP systems when that file or document with hidden data traverses the network. The play for DLP is to use it to detect simple techniques in which people hide data within the metadata fields of Word documents, PDFs, and other common word processing and spreadsheet files.

Non-Destructive Jamming

We can trace one of the first cases of communication jamming to 1904–1905 during the Russo-Japanese conflict. Russian telegraph stations transmitted constant random noise over telegraph channels in order to interrupt communication between Japanese warships. During World War II, the British and US developed methods to evade accurate radar detection by using chaff (small pieces of metal) dropped from aircraft to confuse ground and air-based radar systems. Today, electronic countermeasures are central to any Naval, Air, and Ground campaigns designed to confuse, game, and add stealth to virtually every battlefield situation.

For steganography, some of these fundamental concepts are being applied within network infrastructures. With the advent of Operation Shady Rat, the Alureon Trojan, and many other active malicious applications that employ data hiding methods to evade detection from data leak prevention systems, content filters, and application firewalls. Therefore, the need to consider jamming or disruption methods is essential. As digital images and multimedia files begin to play a larger role in these attack vectors, system operators can apply low cost (to network performance) non-destructive jamming methods. One example of these methods would be a Web gateway equipped with JPEG Jamming (see Figure 11.4).

The process is quite simple:

a. A user makes a URL request via a Web gateway.
b. The gateway forwards the request to the Internet-based URL.
c. The URL responds to the request.
d. The response is intercepted by the Web Gateway and examined.
e. If the response contains a JPEG the response is held, while the JPEG is forwarded to the JPEG Jamming Server.
f. The Jamming server performs sanitization and re-encoding of the JPEG file disrupting any hidden content.

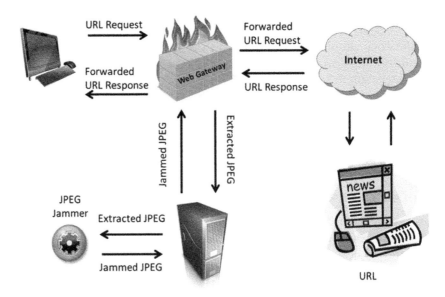

FIGURE 11.4 Non-Destructive Jamming

g. The sanitized JPEG is delivered back to the Web Gateway.

h. The Web Gateway then delivers the sanitized JPEG to the requesting application.

The sanitized JPEG appears unaltered if viewed by the user, however, if the request was made by a malicious application expecting to extract command and control information embedded in the image, this information would have been successfully jammed.

Of course many other forms of jamming would be required as information can be easily concealed in virtually any delivered content (images, multimedia files, Web html, documents, spreadsheets, javascript, etc.).

Endpoint Technologies for detecting Data Hiding

Many vendors provide host-based application blocking capabilities. These capabilities are typically based on a policy setting that defines what applications are either allowed (white listing) or not allowed (black listing). The policy can be defined based on the application name, signature (HASH) or even behavior (for example, system call usage, rights required to execute the application, user permissions, etc.).

Therefore, application blocking could easily be performed against any known steganography application by developing a policy to Not Allow applications of this type to be executed under specific circumstances or by specific users. All you would need is a list of signatures (HASH values) for the set of known steganography applications that you wish to block (and then keep that list updated with new known programs) and you can prevent their execution. These security mechanisms such as McAfee Host Intrusion Prevention System (HIPS) or Symantec Critical System Protection not only provide the blocking mechanisms necessary, but can also relay the attempted action to management consoles or Security Information Event Management systems (SIEM). This provides security personnel with immediate high level warning of potential data leakage of malware infestation alerts (see Table 2).

Many enterprise networks have a vulnerability scanning strategy. For those scanners that allow for custom plug-ins (e.g. Nessus), an administrator could create checks for dlls, executables, and other files related to known data hiding programs. It is important to note that these are not normally identified during network vulnerability scans, but rather during credentialed scans where the scanner logs into the device. Many of the vulnerability scanning products today support NASL (Nessus Attack Scripting Language).[2] The following check

---

[2] Auditing Infected Systems for Viruses for Viruses and Trojans with Nessus—http://blog.
tenablesecurity.com/2009/01/auditing-infected-systems-for-viruses-and-trojans-with-nessus.
html.

Table 11.2 Endpoint Technologies for Detecting Data Hiding Activities

Endpoint or Data-at-Rest	Detection Abilities
Host Intrusion Prevention System (HIPS)	Program abuse (WinHex editing a Word doc)
	Abnormal behaviors
Integrity Monitoring	Changes to files & folders, registry changes, executables
	Changes in database tables & indexes
	Changes in Virtual environments
	Rea time or scheduled
Anti-Virus	Locally installed data hiding programs
eDiscovery	Preserve electronic data and metadata
Vulnerability Scanning (credentialed)	Scanning for known steganography programs, modified dlls inconsistent with latest known dlls, etc.
Mobile Device Management & Security	Detect & Block data hiding and steganography programs (app blocking)
	DLP-like blocking of cut/paste data from one doc into another file, or forwarding E-mail to personal account
Forensics Software	Locally installed data hiding programs
	Evidence of previously installed data hiding programs (unremoved dlls, registery artifacts, etc.)
	Files with embedded content from known data hiding programs
	Files with embedded content from unknown data hiding programs
	Metadata analysis for hidden data

could provide the basis for checking for a registry key made by a steganography program, for example Camouflage:

```
<if>
<condition type: "and">
<custom_item>
type : REGISTRY_SETTING
description : "steganography program Camouflage"
value_type : POLICY_TEXT
reg_key : "HKEY_CURRENT_USER\Software\Camouflage\CamouflageFile\0"
reg_option : CAN_BE_NULL
</custom_item>
```

As we push into the mobile revolution, Mobile Device Management & Security products are positioned very nicely to detect a variety of data hiding and steganography vectors. Many of the products natively detect and can block the downloading of data hiding and steganography mobile applications. Additionally, if the user jailbreaks or roots their phone to circumvent this and other detections, most MDM products also can sever their connections to the corporate network, thus quarantining the user. Furthermore, the administrator can perform a selective or full wipe of the device. MDM products are also starting to show signs of including DLP-like features to prohibit content from being copied from a corporate E-mail and forwarded to a personal E-mail account, or copy/paste into an E-mail or other document file type.

SUMMARY

Today, there is far better success using tools to detect data hiding behaviors on the end user's computer, rather than in-transit. This is a result of tool maturity. Techniques for detecting evidence of hidden data originated with forensic investigators. Therefore, the most mature products are forensic analysis tools for analyzing data-at-rest on imaged suspect computers (see Figure 11.5).

As time progressed and the enterprise had a stronger desire to protect against attacks such as corporate espionage, tools such as anti-virus, host-based intrusion prevention (HIPS), eDiscovery, an integrity monitoring tools enhanced their detection capabilities. Some anti-virus vendors began to scan common hiding locations such as alternate data streams. eDiscovery tools matured to allow administrators to define policies classify certain files and identify their existence on unauthorized desktops. But the Data-at-Rest Live Analysis products have room to mature in terms of detecting evidence of hidden data or data hiding behaviors. For example, HIPS and file integrity monitoring tools

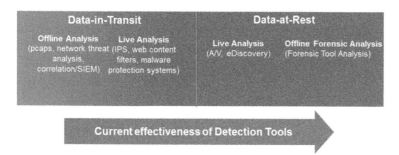

FIGURE 11.5 Effectiveness of Data Hiding Detection Tools

are not tuned out of the box to detect program abuse. If a user opens a PDF document in WinHex and hides data, it's highly likely that these monitoring tools will not flag this abnormal behavior.

Considering the broad arena of data hiding techniques, it would seem to suggest that modeling the behaviors of hiding data versus mapping all of the techniques would be far more effective. Operating system policies could be enhanced and enforced to prevent undesired behaviors. For example, should a normal end user be exhibiting behaviors such as hiding a file in an alternate data stream or volume shadow copy? Should an end user have the ability to install a known steganography program and install it on the computer or mobile device? These behaviors are far easier to detect, control, and prohibit through existing operating system or mobile device management policies.

Many of the scenarios demonstrated in this book should be tested in an enterprise network to test the effectiveness of the network's defense-in-depth technologies. First, this will test the effectiveness (or lack thereof) of each product. The results of the testing can then allow the team to fortify each product through tuning and customizations. And many additionally enforce the need for additional controls or alternative defensive technologies. Apply Dan Farmer's methodology and applying it to data hiding, the team can download a data hiding program and determine if the next generation firewall (NGFW),[3] content filter, anti-virus, malware protection system, and other products in the network detect the downloads. Lists of common steganography programs can be obtained at Dr. Neil Johnson's site at www.jjtc.com/Steganography/tools.[4]html. Mature products should allow the administrator to add these programs to the detection filters.

One or more innocuous steganography program can be installed on a test system to determine the effectiveness of a host-based intrusion prevention system, integrity monitoring, and other data-at-rest monitoring tools. Anything not detected should be modified in their respective policies and retested.

In summary, there seems to be a gap in analyzing for malicious user behaviors on laptops and desktops. For example, should a user be hiding data in a volume shadow copy on their Windows laptop or creating a hidden linux directory on their Mac? Or should a user be editing a Word document in a hex editor to hide additional data? Detection of these behaviors should be incorporated into more security products to prohibit malicious users from circumventing native technologies. Files should be signed to ensure their integrity and authenticity.

---

[3] Next Generation Firewalls for Dummies, by Lawrence C. Miller—Palo Alto Networks.
[4] Steganography Tools, Neil Johnson—http://www.jjtc.com/Security/stegtools.htm.

This applies to Microsoft Word documents, Adobe PDF files, multimedia, etc. Products today have much room for maturity to improve their ability to detect data hiding techniques. This applies to both products that detect data hiding techniques in data-at-rest as well as data-in-transit.

References

Auditing Infected Systems for Viruses and Trojans with Nessus. <http://blog.tenablesecurity.com/2009/01/auditing-infected-systems-for-viruses-and-trojans-with-nessus.html>.

Next Generation Firewalls for Dummies, by Lawrence C. Miller, CISSP Palo Alto Networks

NIJ, Electronic Crime Technology Center of Excellence. <http://www.ectcoe.net/resources/tools>.

Steganography Tools, Neil Johnson. <http://www.jjtc.com/Security/stegtools.htm>.

This page is intentionally left blank

## CHAPTER 12

Futures

INFORMATION IN THIS CHAPTER:

- The Future, and the Past

CONTENTS

THE FUTURE, AND THE PAST

Steganography remains the leader in data hiding techniques by its very nature. In relation to its cousin, cryptography, the very nature of its ability to be hidden and remain hidden until revealed by its recipient differs greatly from cryptography. Data hiding continues to proliferate throughout our daily lives. Ranging from hidden RFIDs in the products we buy, to our computer printers that print hidden identifiable information printed on every page; hidden data touches our lives in so many ways most of us aren't aware of.

As we press further into the 21st century, we are witnessing the explosive growth of mobile devices and wireless communications. We can expect new forms and uses of data hiding to emerge. Unbeknownst to the average user, a picture taken on our smart phone now includes GPS coordinates, camera, and phone serial number information, and other identifiable information hidden within the picture. Wireless communications currently include network identifiers in the headers of the network packets, detailing the originator from which the packets were sent. We expect further proliferation in these areas of ubiquitous mobility.

In terms of military implementations we have already seen legitimate wireless communications and transmissions hidden within a larger number of fake transmissions, so as to throw-off any eavesdropper. For example, in 1942, the Radio Intelligence Division (RID) of the United States Federal Communication Commission (FCC) joined forces with the British Radio Security Service to identify German espionage networks. The equipment included a receiver for collecting signals on a range of frequencies and a

229

Data Hiding. http://dx.doi.org/10.1016/B978-1-59-749743-5.00012-2

"snifter," "a meter that a man could carry in the palm of his hand while inspecting a building to see which apartment a signal came from,"[1] similar to modern day wireless war walking.

The patrolman would scan through the frequencies making note of apparently legitimate transmissions found on every pass for weeks and months, while also noting anomaly signals not present in previous scans. These anomalies were then recorded for detailed review. Great intelligence was collected on the Nazis including the processes by which the Nazi spies traveled around with transmitter-receivers the size of a suitcase using directional antennas and signal power to minimize dispersion. As the analysis progressed, the Allies had collected and deciphered a variety of codes and cipher allowing them to read many of the Nazi messages.

As the Nazis became aware of the Axis tactics, they created their own "Funkspiel." Funkspiel comes from the word "Funk" or radio, and "Spiel" or play. Essentially the Nazis setup decoy radio networks that appeared to be legitimate but were really fabricated information. As the Allies identified networks and read the messages, it caused the Allies to realign their troops and attacks. In a way, the Nazis where manipulating the Allies to understand their intentions or position them for counterattack. This caused the Allies to lose confidence in the intelligence, until the Allies created their own funkspiel to mislead the Nazis.[2] Modern day funkspiels may be developed. These may include legitimate transmissions hidden within fake transmissions or transmissions embedded within transmissions so as to throw-off eavesdroppers.

Future Threats

As we have seen throughout history, beginning with Demaratus in ancient times, to the use of Null Ciphers by the Germans in World War II, to the Russian Spy case[3] and Operation Shady Rat, the use of data hiding and steganography evolves with the times.

When new devices like the iPad and Android appear, new advanced data hiding and steganography threats are quick to respond. And as we have seen with digital images, multimedia files, virtual machines, and operating systems, the evolution of these technologies is constant. With the need for malware creators, bot herders, criminal organizations, terrorists, and nation states to conceal their command and control activities, it is not only likely that steganography and other advanced data hiding methods will expand and evolve—it is a given.

---

[1] The Codebreakers, by David Kahn, p. 526.
[2] The Codebreakers, David Kahn, pp. 526–534.
[3] Russian Spy Ring http://www.theregister.co.uk/2010/06/29/spy_ring_tech/.

Looking toward the future then, the integration of advanced data hiding methods will likely target the following areas in the near term:

- Cloud Computing.
- Virtualization.
- Advanced Streaming Protocols.
- Metadata.
- Databases.
- Wireless Protocols.
- Smartphones & Tablets.

Following these obvious areas of future expansion, we need to examine more closely how advance persistent threats are using data hiding and steganography to conceal their activities. This would not only include Trojans, but would expand to Key Loggers, Botnets, Rootkits, Spyware, Network wired, and wireless sniffers, remote access applications and anti-forensic technologies.

Wireless—The New Frontier

Wireless technologies and protocols continue to grow at an alarming rate. As we've grown accustomed in a short amount of time to ubiquitous mobility. WiFi, Bluetooth, 3G, 4G, and all of the variants of these technologies make us wonder about our ability (or inability) to monitor these technologies for hidden data. There are far less technologies for monitoring these networks for data that may be hidden in the payload or even the protocol headers themselves.

I demonstrated the ability to communicate hidden data in the WiFi protocol by using Beacons as a transport mechanism for data. Originally created by Microsoft Research, Beacon Stuffing[4] is a technique where the Information Element of a WiFi Beacon packet can be used to carry ads distributed to WiFi devices in the neighboring airspace. Think of it as a Kmart "blue light special." A user downloads a mobile app allowing them to receive in-store specials that day while they're at the store. The WiFi network sends them an ad carrier in a Beacon packet from the access point to the user's mobile device, and the app allows them to view the coupon or special.

Applying this method to carry hidden data, we can effectively use the same technique. The Information Element portion of the packet allows for up to 253 of the 256 bytes to be used for "vendor-specific information" (see Figure 12.1).

This modern day SRAC (Short Range Agent Communication) device could be used to send a series of packets carrying a large message that is then reassembled on the recipient's device (see Figure 12.2).

---

[4] Microsoft Research, Beacon Stuffing http://research.microsoft.com/pubs/73482/BeaconStuffing.pdf.

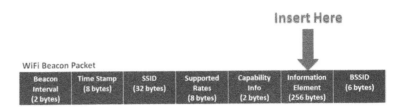

FIGURE 12.1 WiFi Beacon Packet

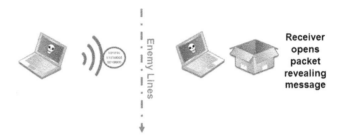

FIGURE 12.2 Stego Stuffing

The original SRAC device was created by the Soviets in 1970's and allowed "messages to be written on a computer to be downloaded onto a small SRAC transmitter. This device, slightly larger than a cigarette pack sends out a low power interrogation signal. When the receiving agent is close enough—about 100 m away—the SRAC transmitter makes contact and "burst" transmits any waiting messages."[5]

I prefer to call this more modern technique "Stego Stuffing" after taking inspiration from Microsoft Research's Beacon Stuffing paper. By taking the results and reassembling them, the recipient can extract and reveal the hidden message. This could be used for a variety of small messages such as lock combinations, Instant Messenger-like messages, etc. A larger message could be encapsulated and sent once, or multiple times using a tool such as aireplay-ng. The possibilities are endless. The following example demonstrates this using Wireshark (see Figure 12.3).

In addition, frequency hopping, nonstandard WiFi channels, and other wireless protocol characteristics can circumvent Wireless IPS detections. Additionally, the example provided above is performed with the recipient device not connected to any wireless network, and purely in promiscuous mode, making

[5] The Spycraft Manual: The Insider's Guide to Espionage Techniques, by Barry Davies and Richard Thomlinson, p. 63.

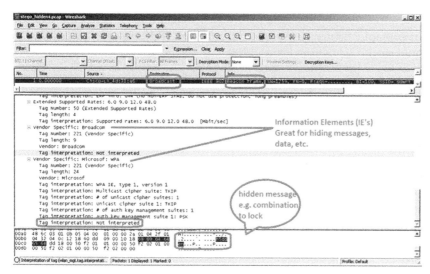

FIGURE 12.3 Wireshark capture of Stego Stuffing

it additionally difficult to detect the activity by detecting neighboring wireless client devices. With the device not connected to any wireless network and by not broadcasting, it's nearly impossible to detect the recipient.

Most enterprises have a plethora of products for their wired networks to create a defense-in-depth strategy. But as we reach the tipping point of mobile devices outnumbering wired devices, we are once again at a disadvantage for detecting hidden data. This is of special concern considering that wireless is the preferred method of communication across enemy lines. Although Wireless Intrusion Prevention Systems are very mature, they're designed more for detecting rogue devices, wireless attacks on other devices, and protocol abuse. But they are not fine-tuned to detect the existence of hidden messages. There is a growing need for wireless detection technologies in this area. We can also expect to see the emergence of more data hiding techniques using wireless protocols including WiFi, Bluetooth, Virtual WiFi, 3G, 4G, etc. The need exists as demonstrated by the recent Russian Spy case where wireless adhoc networks were used to transport secret documents.[6]

Steganography as a Countermeasure

One option in the defense of our systems is to turn the tables on those attacking our systems (insiders or outsiders). By utilizing the capabilities of steganography as a countermeasure we can improve attribution, pedigree and provenance

---

[6] Russian Spy Ring—http://www.theregister.co.uk/2010/06/29/spy_ring_tech/.

of corporate documents, proposals, intellectual property, and even databases that contain Personal Identifiable Information (PII). In a simplified view, this would work as shown in Figure 12.4.

An authorized user creates a document, briefing, spreadsheet, digital image, multimedia file, etc. It is deemed that this document should include a provenance marker. The original object is sent to the Stego-Based Provenance Marker Server. The server secretly embeds hidden markers throughout the object. The markers are embedded in such a way that even when the object is modified or altered the markers remain. This may sound similar to a watermark, however, the content of the markers contain pedigree information (ownership, location, timestamp, description, confidentiality information, expiration, etc.) As the document, image, movie or other digital object is circulated throughout the organization, strategically placed security components can detect the markers and apply policy that would determine distribution, release, access control and integrity

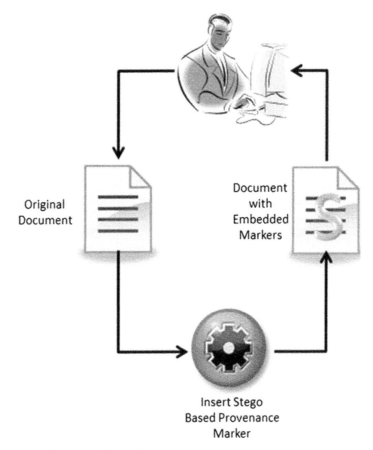

Original Document

Document with Embedded Markers

Insert Stego Based Provenance Marker

FIGURE 12.4 Steganography as a Countermeasure

operations. Documents, images, etc. that do not have provenance markers, could then be scanned and marked based on the trustworthiness and handling. Even host devices could determine, (based on policy again) how digital objects with/without out provenance markers would be handled, quarantined or processed. This is because the hidden markers don't effect the usefulness of the object, (in other words they do not affect the quality of the images, multimedia file, document or database as they are non-intrusive to normal use of the objects).

By examining the usefulness of steganography for such confidentiality, integrity, and trust applications, you increase the overall confidentiality, integrity, and availability of your cyber infrastructure. Much of today's cyber security mechanisms rely on passive detection of threats. This method is becoming more difficult as network and processing speeds increase, and the number of devices and diversity of network traffic evolve. We must provide methods to assist these security mechanisms with a-priori and secure information that will improve the efficiencies of these devices.

Current and Futuristic Combined Threats

Data hiding threats are expected to continue to evolve in more sophisticated ways to avoid detection. Some of these methods combine two or more of these techniques (see Figure 12.5).

- *Polymorphic*—Much like virus, data hiding programs can self-mutate when hiding the data so as to throw-off signature based detections (e.g. Hydan which hides data in executables in different ways at run-time).
- *Multidimensional*—This form of data hiding applies multiple techniques or steps to hide data. In one such case, the data is first hidden using an LSB method within the file. That file is then hidden in a Stealth Alternate Data Stream or Volume Shadow Copy.
- *Dispersion*—Some tools utilize methods to hide data (or disperse) across multiple carrier files or transmissions. In addition, the approach may also add decoy files or transmissions with no hidden data to throw-off targeted analysis and detection (e.g. OpenPuff).

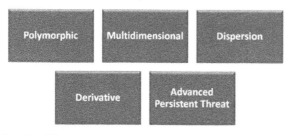

FIGURE 12.5 Combined Threats

- *Derivative*—One form of the derivative technique is where a data is hidden in a file, while modifying other innocuous files so as to throw-off the investigator (e.g. "touching" multiple Linux files to change dates and times on a large quantity of files, or modifying the checksums on a large number of files).
- *Advanced Persistent Threat*—Although this is a broad definition, one recent example with Operation Shady RAT involved routinely obtaining images with hidden data that included the latest command and control URLs or IP addresses.

As covered in the Mitigation Strategies chapter, detection technologies that identify behavioral patterns and heuristics related to data hiding activities are the best adaptive technologies for these evolving combined threats. Bottomline, combined threats should be mitigated using combined detection techniques.

SUMMARY

As we look back on the story of Demaratus and how he carved that secret message into the wood of the wax tablet in order to avoid detections by the sentries of the day, one has to wonder how far have we actually come in 2,500 years. Recently, we gave a presentation to a group of some of the best cyber security minds in the world, working to protect the assets of large private and public organizations around the globe. We asked the following simple question.... "If someone or some application hides information inside a digital image and then E-mails that image as an attachment via the normal channels with the most modern sentries available today in place, how many of these messages would be blocked?" Essentially, repeating the message exfiltration that Demaratus successfully executed over 2500 years ago.

Not a single hand was raised.

Index

Note: Page numbers followed by "f" and "t" indicate figures and tables respectively

This page is intentionally left blank

This page is intentionally left blank

This page is intentionally left blank

Printed and bound by CPI Group (UK) Ltd, Croydon, CR0 4YY

03/10/2024

01040343-0006